JULIA BUCKROYD trained as a counsellor at the Department of Extra-Mural Studies at the University of London. Since then her counselling career has taken her from a neurosurgery unit, to a bereavement counselling service, and onto her present position as a student counsellor at the London Contemporary Dance School.

She was educated at St Andrews University, McMaster University in Canada, and at Cambridge University. She has written extensively on a wide variety of subjects, ranging from counselling, to dance, to Scottish history.

D1340997

EATING YOUR HEART OUT

THE EMOTIONAL MEANING OF EATING DISORDERS

JULIA BUCKROYD

An OPTIMA book

© Julia Buckroyd 1989

First published in 1989 by
Macdonald Optima, a division of
Macdonald & Co. (Publishers) Ltd

A member of Maxwell Pergamon Publishing Corporation plc

All rights reserved

No part of this publication may be reproduced,
stored in a retrieval system, or transmitted,
in any form or by any means without the prior
permission in writing of the publisher, nor be
otherwise circulated in any form of binding or
cover other than that in which it is published
and without a similar condition including this
condition being imposed on the subsequent
purchaser.

British Library Cataloguing in Publication Data

Buckroyd, Julia
   Eating your heart out.
   1. Women. Eating behaviour. Psychological aspects
   I. Title
   155.6'33

   ISBN 0-356-17088-8

Photoset in Century Schoolbook
by Leaper & Gard Ltd, Bristol, England

Printed and bound in Great Britain by
The Guernsey Press Co. Ltd., Guernsey, Channel Islands.

Macdonald & Co. (Publishers) Ltd
66-73 Shoe Lane
Holborn
London EC4P 4AB

CONTENTS

For dearest B
without whom not

PREFACE

Ten years ago as an academic with pastoral responsibility for up to fifty women college students at any one time, I began to be aware of the prevalence of eating disorders among female students. My first conscious acknowledgement of this problem among the women whose welfare was my concern came when a worried landlady phoned to tell me that one of them seemed to be surviving on about 300 calories a day. It was the beginning of a long-term attempt to understand problems with food, eating, weight and size. That process continued through my decision to leave the academic world and retrain as a counsellor and has developed over the past five years in my work as student counsellor at London Contemporary Dance School as well as with the clients I see privately.

During this time I have had ample opportunity to reflect on my own eating behaviour and my own use of food. I have become aware of how, at particularly stressful times during my life, I have become what I should now describe as anorexic and lost significant amounts of weight. I have also been able to recognise what I now think of as many anorexic episodes when some disturbing event or experience has made me vow not to eat for the next day or few. I have also had to acknowledge that since my teens there have been times when I have binged and then vomited and many more times when I have just binged, especially late at night when I have not been able to sleep. I count myself happy that these ways of trying to deal with emotional pain have never taken over my life for all that long and have never been clinically diagnosed; the longest anorexic time lasted a little less than a year. However, I also know that I am still capable of eating nothing because my heart hurts or of eating more than I want for the same reason. I am glad that it is now some years since I have made myself sick. It has taken me a long time to feel kinder to myself and to be more accepting of my pain.

This book, therefore, is not written from the position of someone who is happy in the knowledge that she is not troubled by these difficult problems. I have some idea of how much anguish eating disorders can cause the sufferer. When I first began to read books on the subject in the late seventies I was very put off by the distant, lofty, superior and often punishing tone of much that was written by their usually male, often medical, authors. Anorexics were labelled sly and deceitful, bulimics disgusting, compulsive eaters greedy and untruthful. I found something voyeuristic in their descriptions of binges or bulimic episodes. Their concentration on medical diagnoses, physical symptoms and violent solutions — operations, administrations of drugs, forced feeding, behavioural conditioning programmes, aversion therapy — seemed to me then, and does now, unlikely to help women who are seriously disturbed to regain a sense of themselves and a respect and love for their own bodies. It is my experience that people with eating disorders are all too ready to insult and attack themselves both physically and verbally. Further attacks from those who want to help seem unlikely to be useful.

At the basis of any therapeutic endeavour there needs to develop an alliance, a trust, a co-operation, a mutual respect. We none of us want to have good done to us, at the expense of our dignity and our pride. I have tried to incorporate these ideals in these pages. You, the reader, are in the end responsible for yourself and your own behaviour. You may need some help, but you are the one who has to want it and to take it. Nobody can make you better against your will. This book invites you to take an active part in looking at your own behaviour and in considering how your own experiences are reflected in what is described.

Eating disorders are now the commonest symptom with which women in our society express their distress. The scale of the problem is enormous, especially at a sub-clinical level. Perhaps not all that many are so ill that they find their way to a doctor; that does not mean that they do not have a problem. When eating disorders were perceived as affecting only a small group within the population then it might have made sense (though I doubt it) to explain them by reference to one theory. The one that was most often suggested was that women with eating disorders had problems with growing up and especially with their sexuality. This may be true for some, but not for all. Most recently feminists have suggested that eating disorders are women's unconscious response to the social role in which society places them. I respect feminists' work enormously and think it is by far the most exciting and creative work done in recent years, but I still do not believe that all eating disorders can be understood by reference to this, or any, one theory.

What I have attempted here is to present a *range* of ways of understanding and thinking about the emotional meaning of eating disorders. It is your role to consider where you fit in. There may be more than one way of thinking about your difficulties. Perhaps none of what follows will match your situation exactly, but I hope you will get some clues about what is going on when you find yourself using your eating behaviour as a means of expressing your emotional pain.

The experience on which this book is written is very largely my work as a counsellor working with young women between the age of 16 and 25. This group has been multi-racial, although predominantly white, and across a socio-economic spectrum from working class to upper middle class. It has included a few men, but only a few and all of them young; and a few older middle-class women, but only a few. I have not worked with people in their early teens. My experience, therefore, has the limitations imposed by the restrictions of the sample of the populations with whom I have worked.

The names and details of the case histories have been altered to make the people concerned unidentifiable, except perhaps to themselves. In some instances a number of similar stories have been put together and in others one story has been presented as several separate histories. This has been done to protect further the identity of those with whom I have worked, as well as to illustrate what I am saying. Some of the histories presented I have learned of from colleagues. Some of my clients have known that I was writing this book and have kindly offered me diaries, poems and other writing to use. I would like to thank them for their generosity. I would also like to record my respect for those sufferers from eating disorders who, with great courage, have shared their pain and distress. What I know about the subject I have learned largely from them.

I would also like to express my thanks to those without whom this book would not have been written: first of all to my colleagues at London Contemporary Dance School. My time in the school as student counsellor is made more enjoyable by their friendship and support. I am given space, time and opportunity to develop counselling work and attitudes within the school and although my ideas and activities do not always meet with their agreement, they are respected. I owe a particular debt of gratitude to the Principal of the school, Richard Ralph, and to the body-conditioning teacher, Sonia Noonan.

I would further like to thank my friends, teachers and mentors within the counselling and therapeutic world. My retraining and development as a counsellor has been greatly assisted by their help and support. I would particularly like to mention Ellen Noonan, Gerald Wooster, John Foskett, John Boreham and Eileen Smith. I am grateful to those who have accompanied me on my journey inwards and have enabled my emotional growth, especially to Sadie Gillespie. To my husband Peter Buckroyd with this book, as with others, I owe an enormous amount. Without his sustained practical help and continuing support and encouragement this book would not have been written.

SECTION ONE

1
EATING DISORDERS ARE NOT ABOUT FOOD

We need to understand what a woman is saying when she uses her body to express difficult emotional issues. We need to understand why it is safer to say, 'I need to go on a diet' than 'I feel hurt or upset or in conflict.'

Susie Orbach, *Fat is a Feminist Issue*

This book is written for those who are unhappy about the way they use food. It is partly for those who find it hard to eat. Those are the people who get hungry but who don't want to eat. Perhaps they feel they can't. And there are people who would rather be thin than satisfy hunger. It is for those people especially who are afraid that they cannot eat, and afraid that the problem is out of control. And it is for those who sometimes with part of themselves would like to be able to eat and not be frightened that they will eat and eat until they are fat.

However, it is also written for those people who eat too much, those who eat when they are not hungry, when they are already full, when they no longer want or need to eat any more. It is for those people who eat all the time and hate themselves for it. And it is for those who sometimes with part of themselves would like to be able to eat only when they are hungry or when they want to eat.

This book is also for those undereaters or overeaters, starving or bingeing, who feel the terrible need to get rid of what they have put inside themselves, however much or little. Those are the people who leave the table to go to the bathroom and stick their fingers down their throats and those who give themselves laxatives, enemas or diuretics so that they force food and drink out of their systems before it can be used and absorbed by their bodies. It is for those purgers and vomiters who sometimes with part of themselves would like to be able to eat without the terrible foreknowledge that they will have to get rid of it soon afterwards.

Nor must the families and friends and helpers of all those people with eating difficulties be overlooked. There is something terrible about watching someone who is precious to you deliberately hurting and harming herself. It is even worse when you realise that the behaviour is out of control and that it causes the sufferer tremendous emotional pain. Perhaps reading this book will help them understand better what is going on with the one they love, and how best to help and support her if she decides to try and get well.

But this book is also written for those very many women who are not so fat or so thin or so preoccupied with food that it has taken over their lives, but who, from time to time, suffer episodes of anorexia or compulsive eating or bulimia. At an all-day workshop for women involved with the care of those with eating disorders, participants were asked to do an exercise designed to encourage them to reflect upon their own misuse of food. This, when you think about it, has startling implications. The assumption is that women looking after those with eating disorders will themselves have sufficient personal experience of misusing food to understand their patients' problems. Nobody objected to this assumption. Indeed many participants found it useful to reflect upon their own eating behaviour. Yet the implication is that in this (admittedly self-selected) group of professionals 100 per cent will have adequate experience of food misuse in their own lives to help them appreciate their patients' difficulties.

HOW BIG A PROBLEM IS IT?

In a study of a group of women at college, 90 per cent of the group had used 'unnatural' means of weight control over the past year. It seems that the vast majority of modern women in the Western world find themselves, from time to time, misusing food and are anxious and bothered about that fact.

Although we live in an age where eating disorders are exceedingly common, many books on the subject start off by saying that there is nothing new about all this and that problems around food have been known for a very long time. It is certainly true that throughout recorded history there have been many people, frequently but not always women, who have used and misused food to such a remarkable degree that the fact has been noted. What is new, and what this book is concerned to point out, is that eating disorders now affect a very high proportion of women.

Problems with food, with eating, and with what that implies for size, weight and shape, are now endemic in the female population in our culture. The traditional psycho-analytic response to this situation has been to identify these problems as indications of difficulties with sexuality. Feminist writers have extended this argument and have suggested that since eating disorders are overwhelmingly a female complaint, the root of the problem lies in the way women see themselves and the pressures they are under in our culture to achieve a certain size and shape. Both of these are very useful approaches and they will be discussed later in detail. However I would like to assert that the meaning of an eating disorder to any particular woman cannot be presumed, but remains to be discovered.

Increasingly I come to think that the significance of eating disorders lies in the fact that in our culture it is the symptom which has real meaning for women. What lies behind the distress signalled by eating disorders needs to be explored and will differ from woman to woman and may also differ within that person's own history. Just as hysteria was the common symptom of distress in Freud's Vienna at the end of the last century, and is now increasingly rare, so eating disorders are becoming, and perhaps have already become, an important way that contemporary women signal emotional pain.

The idea of a symptom or a mode of behaviour belonging to one gender or another is not new. Indeed 'hysteria' in Freud's patients was largely a female complaint. Depression is also a symptom which is far more common in women than in men. On the other hand, alcohol misuse, violence and delinquency are problems (and symptoms of distress as well as crimes) overwhelmingly of men. It is a commonplace that men very often turn their distress outwards and against others, while women very often turn it inwards and against themselves. Eating disorders may well be the latest way that women have found of turning their pain inwards and acting it out on themselves.

So a major concern in this book is the fact that eating disorders are extremely common, especially among women. And central to this is the argument that not only is this something new and perhaps culturally influenced, but that it is also culturally understood. It makes sense, in other words, for our society that people have eating disorders. What I want to add to that, and what has already been implied, is that eating disorders are above all not only about eating. They are a signal from ourselves to ourselves and also perhaps to anyone else who has eyes to see and ears to hear. *What* those meanings may be will be further explored later.

THE EMOTIONAL ROOT OF EATING DISORDERS

Gross disorders of size or eating behaviour have quite often been observed and noted in the past. They have been met with puzzlement, curiosity, admiration, rage and attempts at understanding. In women, anorexia has been more frequently identified. In *Holy Anorexia* Rudolph Bell describes how in the Middle Ages what we should now understand as anorexic behaviour — self-starvation —

was regarded in religious young women as a sign of holiness and asceticism. It was noticed in the seventeenth century where a sufferer was described as 'a skeleton only clad with skin', but it was not until the nineteenth century that the syndrome was recognised by the medical profession and given a name. These nineteenth-century doctors began to be certain that anorexia had an emotional basis: 'a morbid mental state . . . hysteria'. Although there have been a number of suggested physical causes for anorexia — most recently the possibility of zinc deficiency — there has also been a consistent development over the intervening century since anorexia was first diagnosed and named of the idea that the illness has an emotional basis which demands understanding and attention. This, however, is an exceptionally difficult task and often meets with failure.

In most cases the meaning of the eating behaviour is not obvious even to the sufferer. The meanings that come most readily to mind usually prove not very helpful to understanding what is going on. Janet French was a dancer whose story was written up in the *Evening Standard Magazine* in February 1988. She had been dancing full time since the age of 11 and was obviously talented. In the face of tremendous competition she won a place in a ballet company at the age of 17. Several years later, at the age of 22, her parents noticed a severe weight loss which Janet explained to them as the result of having been told to lose weight for her dancing. She continued to lose weight and this was then explained as the result of three members of the company having been told to leave because they were overweight. In other words, the meaning that Janet was giving to her weight loss was that it was in response to the demands of the job. Keeping the job, she was implying, was worth any amount of starvation.

The difficulty about this account of her behaviour lies in the fact that it has a certain amount of truth in it. It is the case that since about the 1960s there has been a fashion for ballet dancers (and to a lesser extent dancers generally) to be extremely thin. However, it is also possible to see by reference to photographs and paintings that this *is* recent aesthetic preference. Undoubtedly Janet was under great pressure to keep her weight well below the norm for her age and height. In 1985, however, Janet lost her job because she had become too weak to be able to dance. Obviously, then, whatever were the reasons for her anorexia it was not simply that Janet wanted above all else to be able to dance. In the end her anorexia lost her her job. What was tragic is that it also lost her her life.

Sometimes after the event the sufferers can tell us something of what the illness meant to them. Anna developed anorexia just at the moment when several important things happened in her life: her best friend went abroad, perhaps forever; her mother had a hysterectomy; Anna herself left home for the first time to go to college. Yet none of these things seemed to lie at the root of her illness and talking about them did not help. Gradually with the support of her family and a circle of concerned helpers, she made a spontaneous recovery over a period of more than two years. When she was about to leave college after three years, she went to see the counsellor who had originally tried to help, and talked about the illness. At that distance she felt she could understand something of what had been going on. She had been a very lively and adventurous adolescent, exploring her world and experimenting with life. Her family trusted her, felt she could take care of herself, better indeed than her less adventurous sister. Anna began to get frightened. She wasn't sure that she was in control of her sexuality, of her wildness, or of her wish to experiment. Would she be able to take care of herself in the big city where her college was situated? Perhaps not. And then what would happen? Just at that moment of anxiety her mother was operated on and her best friend left. Maybe those things felt like warnings or punishments. In any case, Anna knew that she felt the urgent need to put the brakes on her development. Looking back on her anorexia she said that she felt that she had been standing still for three years. Her social life had come to an end as well as her sexual relationships. In fact she said that she hadn't been any use to anyone. But in that time something had changed. She felt able to resume her development as a person. Her need for time out was over. So for Anna there was meaning in her anorexia and it had served a vital emotional purpose, although at enormous cost.

ANOREXIA

Anorexia is the most extreme of eating disorders and the most life threatening. For that reason it has attracted a great deal of attention. The idea that its increasing commonness is new and also that it is an illness with emotional meaning was advanced several years ago by one of the most distinguished pioneers in the attempt to understand the subject, Hilde Bruch. In *The Golden Cage*, a book that has now become a classic, she put together the understanding of the subject she had gained after years of clinical experience. Bruch wrote at a time when anorexia affected young middle-class teenagers from prosperous backgrounds. Nowadays it affects women of all ages and all classes. Yet much that Bruch wrote contained the ideas that have been so much expanded since. One of her helpful contributions has been her observation that people who starve (themselves) do not behave like ordinary rational human beings. Their starvation has biological effects which makes them think and behave in strange ways. In the treatment of anorexia, therefore, there must be some space for attention to the symptom as well as to its underlying cause.

In practice it is extremely difficult to get the balance right between thinking about the code message that the eating behaviour tries to convey and responding to the practical problems which the way food is being misused will create. In a way it is much easier to respond to the eating behaviour, whether anorexia or any other eating disorder. After all, there it is straight in front of us. For that reason most of this book attempts to deal with the other half of the problem: what is it that makes people use food in such painful and unhappy ways?

COMPULSIVE EATING

Compulsive eating and obesity also have a long history, just like anorexia, and similarly they are nowadays dramatically on the increase in our culture. What is more, too many anorexics have at some time been overweight for it to be likely that anorexia and obesity are totally different things. It seems much more probable that they are opposite sides of the same coin, and both of them variations on the misuse of food.

Barbara was an American college student spending some months in England on an exchange programme. The family with whom she was living gradually became aware that she was eating very little and after some weeks approached the administrator of the programme to report that as far as they knew she was eating no more than 300 calories a day. Other students had already noticed Barbara's weight loss and had reported their anxieties, so it was not long before Barbara was challenged on the subject and after a while she agreed to see a counsellor. It then became clear that what had been noticed in England was only part of the picture. Barbara's weight fluctuated all the way from 140 lbs (63 kg) when she was at home down to less than 90 lbs (40.5 kg) when she was at college. Food, eating and body size had become a continual torment for her, and one in which she no longer had any sense of her 'real' size or of how much was a good amount to eat. Her natural sense of how much she should eat had completely deserted her. At 140 lbs (63 kg) she was considerably overweight for her age and height; at 90 lbs (40.5 kg) she was considerably under.

But if we are talking about the way obesity has been noticed historically, it has usually been the fat men of history whose enormous size or enormous appetites have been recorded: the king who 'died of a surfeit of Lampreys'; King Henry VIII whose portraits and armour reveal his girth; the Prince Regent who was so fat that he was unable to climb the stairs at his little retreat at Kenwood. Then there are the fat men of literature:

Falstaff, Billy Bunter; and the fat men of legend: the entries in the *Guinness Book of Records*. Again there is a strange mixture of feelings aroused by these extraordinary figures: admiration, disgust, ridicule. Perhaps even less than with anorexia is there reason sought for these extreme cases of obesity. The monstrous discomfort might in itself lead us to seek to account for this condition. Yet the reasons given are often the most trivial and unilluminating: 'I just like my food too much; I'm just made that way; it runs in the family'.

Take, for example, the fat man of what used to be the Liberal Party, Sir Cyril Smith, MP for Rochdale, the butt of endless jokes and comments, repeatedly appearing on television screens as he awkwardly levers himself out of a car or attempts to touch (or even see) his toes. Recently he suffered a heart attack and announced his intention to retire from politics. So here is a career politician forced to retire from what he evidently likes to do by his own size. There seems a clear parallel with Janet, the anorexic danger, and equally such behaviour so defies ordinary logic that it demands an answer, a reason.

What is more, there is a huge industry built on the back of this incomprehension. Millions of pounds are spent on calorie-reduced products, on diet books, classes, regimes designed to enable people to reach or retain an ordinary size and weight. What is generally acknowledged is that virtually all of the weight lost by these systems is regained. Yet the obvious conclusion that people attain the weight they do, become the size they are, for some very good emotional meaning, is neglected. Certainly it would not be good for business if it were generally understood that buying aids to weight loss is most unlikely to be a useful or helpful thing to do. Yet I think that we should do ourselves this much credit and believe that we would not have made ourselves the shape and size we are without very good reason. Moreover, it will be obvious to many of us that any weight or size alteration is likely to be temporary unless something changes inside us.

Elizabeth Taylor, a woman who lives in the public eye if

ever a woman did, has written what amounts to an auto-biography of her size, weight and shape changes over the years. It is a depressing catalogue of weight lost and regained. However, eventually Elizabeth Taylor saw the light:

> But since I finally made up my mind to do something about my weight I have never wavered from my goal. The difference this time was that I was also willing to face the emotional needs behind my obesity and do something about those problems too. (*Elizabeth Takes Off*, Macmillan, 1988).

Feminist writers think that weight loss for women is a massive con trick visited upon women by means of the advertising industry which equates thinness with sexual attractiveness and holds up unrealistic ideals for size and shape to women (and also, though they do not say so, for men). However, we would be deceiving ourselves if we did not acknowledge that there are also large numbers of overweight and obese people in our society.

It is true that some women would only feel really thin enough if they regained their prepubescent weight — a goal that, fortunately for our health, is probably unattainable for most of us. But it is also true that many women feel uncomfortable for practical reasons at the size they are and would like to lose some weight. The mystery to them is why they cannot, or why if they do they so rapidly regain the weight that they have lost. Catherine in her late thirties was considerably plumper than she wanted to be. At a time in her life when her morale was high and she felt able to be the person she wanted to be, she gradually and in a moderate and determined sort of way lost weight until she felt herself to be a comfortable size and weight. Within a year she had put it all back on again. She was amazed and angry at herself. It had taken so much determination to get the weight off; how was it that, without consciously intending to do so, she had regained it within so short a space of time? She knew better than anyone that there had to be a reason for such unsatisfying behaviour. It seems that many women in our society use being over-weight as some kind of message to themselves and perhaps also to others.

BULIMIA

If anorexia and compulsive eating have long recorded histories, even though they might be infinitely more common now, what does appear to be quite new is the most painful and distressing of all eating disorders, buli-mia — the bingeing and purging or vomiting that so many food misusers find their way to. No one can keep anorexia or compulsive eating a secret for all that long; the physical effects become visible to anyone who cares to look. But bulimia is the most secret, the most shameful, the most isolating and desolate of all food misuse. Its effects can be very serious physically but are rarely seen by the outsider. It remains a private torment.

WHY SOME PEOPLE MISUSE FOOD

Our concern here is to try and understand what the misuse of food, whatever form it takes, might mean to the individual. The whole of the book rests on the idea that the way we use food does have meaning, even though that meaning might be far from obvious, and not consciously known to the sufferer. It is instead of something; it is instead of feeling, or knowing, or understanding something that feels too difficult or frightening or unacceptable. It is designed to protect us from what we suspect about ourselves. Eating disorders are very preoccupying — we intend them to be; we need them to be, otherwise they would fail in their protective function. And the more frightening that hidden, unknown, suspected something is, the more resolutely we will cling on to our eating disorder. One of the terrible things about eating disorders is that it is very hard for the sufferer to believe that beginning to think and feel and understand what it might be about will not be worse than the pain of the condition itself. Often it seems as though, however painful and upsetting the eating disorder is, the prospect of reflecting upon its meaning is even more painful — in fact impossible. It is for that reason that eating disorders often go on for years and become a way of life.

What is more, it is probably true that there are some difficult things to be known or understood by the food misuser. There *is* something that needs attention, needs to be dealt with; some part of our experience, of our history, some unfinished business. It is unlikely to be very agreeable or very easy or we would not have needed to misuse food rather than let ourselves know about it. But we pay a very high price for the decision not to know. We stunt our development as people, just as Anna brought her life to a standstill with her three years of anorexia. We cheat ourselves of the human possibilities there might be for us.

Diana was a young woman brought up in conditions of extreme maltreatment and deprivation. Yet she had considerable talent as a dancer. Against all the odds she began to develop that talent but after three years of training she first developed anorexia and then bulimia. For her there were all sorts of terrible things about her past that she did not want to know. She could not keep them out of her dreams, but she could keep them out of her life during the day because she thought of nothing but food — how much, how little, when, what sort, how to get it out of her body once she had put it inside. Diana did not enjoy her eating disorder — it was a constant torment to her — but she resolutely maintained that the awful things that had happened to her, her present loneliness, her fear of people, were not important or worth thinking about. The only thing 'wrong' with her was her eating disorder. All she needed was some help with that. She got some help with that — nutritional advice, medical support — but nothing changed. She said sadly that she could not imagine ever being able to live without her preoccupation. But in the meantime so great was her absorption in the ins and outs of food and eating and weight and body size that she stopped dancing. The one really good and positive thing in her life was being destroyed.

We most of us do not have so terrible a history to deal with as Diana, nor are we so totally absorbed in our food misuse that we bring our lives to a standstill, yet even so we waste our lives and our possibilities. Emma was a capable young woman in her late twenties who held down a responsible job and lived an energetic social life. However, she was very frightened of men and found it impossible to accept offers of dates from men although she would liked to have done so. Besides she had found a way of not worrying about that part of her life by worrying about her weight instead. Over a period of six years or so she steadily put on weight and was much heavier than she wanted to be. She had tried innumerable diets but had always abandoned them or put back the weight she had lost. When she began to dare to think through her feelings about men she also began to lose weight and to be freed from her preoccupation with it.

The thing about eating disorders is that they change the currency. Something that belongs to our emotional life, that is about feelings, is being expressed physically by means of behaviour. It is a symptom that simultaneously reveals and conceals. We are using a language that is difficult to translate, difficult for us and usually impossible for other people (or why would they say such things as 'I don't know why you don't eat a bit less/more/more sensibly'?). We believe somewhere inside our heads that we are protecting ourselves from something dreadful by our eating disorders; we think we have found a way of coping with what otherwise seems unmanageable. Instead we create for ourselves a much worse problem by creating a ritual behaviour whenever the world gets too frightening.

Initially the eating disorder is not the problem — we intend it to be the answer to the problem — but it can *become* the problem very quickly. After all, if you lose your job (or in some terrible cases your life) your solution to the problem is hardly brilliant. Even at a much less serious level staying at home counting calories and worrying about your weight and what you have eaten, what you are eating or what you intend to eat does not rate highly as a rewarding way to spend time.

If you suffer from eating disorders and have read thus far there is, however, something on your side, and that is your own curiosity about yourself and a certain amount of motivation to live your life differently. This book is an attempt to help you think about what it might be that you are trying to express or hide or otherwise deal with by means of your eating behaviour. If there were not a part of you willing to try, you would not have got this far. That is not to say that getting better and changing is an easy matter. It is not, for any of us. We all have very mixed feelings about giving up what has become our way of doing things. But at the very beginning I said that this book was for people who are unhappy about the way they use food. You have that on your side to help you — your creative discontent with the way you do things at the moment.

Of course we can all postpone changing. We can hope that things will get better all by themselves without us having to put any thought or effort into making it happen. Most of us long for a magic wand which will change the way things are for us. Unfortunately there are no magic wands and sooner or later we have to take responsibility for the way we live our lives. Sadly if we don't want to get better, at least with a bit of us, nobody can make us. As Anna said when she thought about her three years of anorexia: 'While I didn't want to get better, it didn't matter what anyone said.'

It is also important to recognise, however, the power of habit. The last chapters offer some ideas on how to confront your habitual way of doing things. You may feel like turning to them first and ignoring everything that comes between, but unless you can make some sense of what you are trying to say by your eating behaviour, a full frontal assault on the behaviour itself is unlikely to be much help. After all, if it was that simple you would have done it long ago.

Finally, let me add a few words on what the book does not attempt to do. It does not include a description of eating disorders, or of their diagnosis, or of their physical effects. Nor is it a manual of practical suggestions about how to cope. This is partly because such information is readily available elsewhere and from people better qualified in those areas of expertise, but also because it is not relevant here. The only diagnosis you need is your *own* dissatisfaction with the way you use food. There is, of course, a place for those other kinds of information and some ideas about how to get that kind of help are included in later chapters.

2
WHAT DO YOU THINK OF WHEN YOU THINK OF FOOD?

One day in winter, on my return home, my mother, seeing that I was cold, offered me some tea, a thing I did not ordinarily take . . . She sent for one of those squat, plump little cakes called 'petites madeleines', which look as though they have been moulded in the fluted valve of a scallop shell. And soon . . . I raised to my lips a spoonful of the tea in which I had soaked a morsel of the cake. No sooner had the warm liquid mixed with the crumbs touched my palate than a shudder ran through me and I stopped, intent upon the extraordinary thing that was happening to me. An exquisite pleasure had invaded my senses, something isolated, detached with no suggestion of its origin . . .

And suddenly the memory revealed itself. The taste was that of the little piece of madeleine which on Sunday mornings at Combray . . . my aunt Leonie used to give me, dipping it first in her own cup of tea . . .

And as soon as I had recognised the taste of the piece of madeleine . . . (although I did not yet know and must long postpone the discovery of why this memory made me so happy) immediately the old grey house upon the street, where her room was, rose up like a strange set . . . and the good folk of the village and their little dwellings and the parish church and the whole of Combray and its surroundings, taking shape and solidity, sprang into being, town and gardens alike, from my cup of tea.

Marcel Proust, *Remembrance of Things Past*

Although I have stressed the fact that eating disorders are not about food and that I am concerned to explore what lies behind them, yet it is important to pay some attention to why we might choose this way of expressing our inner selves. For each of us food and eating have a long history and a lifetime of meaning. We can probably begin to find some clues about why we use food in the way we do in the story of our experience of it. In this chapter I want to trace some of our memories of and associations to food during the course of our development. Your part in this process is to recreate your own history and see if you can glimpse some of the inner logic behind your use of food now.

EARLY EXPERIENCES OF FOOD

Good feeding experiences as babies are important because they leave us with memory traces of blissful states which we may later try to recapture. We come into the world totally dependent on our caregivers for our life to continue, but also the vast majority of us are ready to play our part by being able and willing to suck. The baby is hungry, the food appears, the baby sucks and is satisfied. There are some mothers and babies for whom it is that simple some of the time. Perhaps for most of us there are some times when it is that easy, that good. The image of a satisfied, contented baby going off to sleep in its mother's arms is a powerful symbol of total happiness, total security. Maybe for most of us there is some residual memory of blissful fullness and physical comfort.

However, for many the early experiences of food, of hunger, of eating, are not always or even often very straightforward. It takes confidence to feed a tiny baby well, and in our western culture mothers are often not very confident. We have, for instance, became so anxious about our ability to feed our babies from our own breasts that the *majority* of us do not even try to do so. The reason we give is that we do not know how much the baby is getting. We would rather trust a bottle full of reconstituted modified cows' milk that what we ourselves produce.

There is also the fact that we do not always match the baby's need for food soon enough, quickly enough, accurately enough to prevent distress, and it is now half a century since it was first recognised by Melanie Klein what agony that sense of acute hunger arouses in the baby. Hunger is something it cannot name, cannot understand or account for, but only suffer. And that suffering probably induces panic, terror, a violent physical experience perhaps like being torn apart. Most of us adults have experienced hunger acute enough to cause us pain, maybe even panic, but we have a whole world of understanding into which to fit those feelings and with which to help us cope with them. The baby has no such containing framework.

Very few of us can consciously remember those early feeding experiences. We want to believe that they have no effect on us, but it seems very likely that the intensity of that feeling experience remains with us in some preconscious, non-verbal way. For those who misuse food these earliest experiences may well be one element in later difficulties. Charlene had been among those babies who actually experienced starvation. Her mother was simply not equal to the fierce demands of looking after a baby. Charlene was kept alive with ice lollies, until at six weeks she was taken from her mother and put into care. As a young adult Charlene became a compulsive eater who was never full enough, never satisfied.

Of course, that is not the whole story. As baby's experience of being fed is also the experience of being loved, held, taken care of, protected. Missing out on one means missing out on the other experiences too. Charlene's compulsive eating was not only the endless attempt to undo the real physical neglect twenty years earlier, but also the attempt to repair the emotional hurt and damage. It is easy to see in this case how hopeless an enterprise that was; perhaps Charlene's hurts could be healed by better experience of being loved, but certainly they could not be healed by compulsive eating.

For some of us of a certain generation, there was the difficulty that our mothers were taught to disregard their natural urges to pick us up and feed us when we cried and were hungry. Truby King was the male author of manuals of infant care who urged mothers to believe that it was actually harmful for babies to be fed at other than strict four-hourly intervals, however much they cried, and that babies should not be handled more than strictly necessary. The suffering of a sensitive mother who believed such nonsense is surely equal only to the suffering of the baby who received such treatment. These babies must have the most terrible early physical and emotional experience of the pangs of hunger.

Another major event in our infant experience of feeding is weaning. There is so much conflicting advice and so many pressures on mothers now that it is exceedingly difficult for them to attend to the baby's development and to select the right moment for a move away from milk to solids. Some mothers breastfeed for the six weeks that it is said that human milk conveys antibodies to the child and then switch to a bottle with solids. Some give milk for the six months that the baby's natural iron supplies are said to last and then introduce solids. Some read what has been said about the possibility of triggering gluten allergy by feeding cereals too soon and begin solid feeding with puréed fruit and so on. Many mothers return to work after the statutory six weeks maternity leave and that necessarily puts an end to breastfeeding if not to bottle feeding.

Very few mothers have the freedom — practical or emotional — and the confidence to wait and see what their baby wants and needs and when it will happily, and with curiosity and pleasure, begin to explore the interesting possibilities of mixed feeding, in the way that D.W. Winnicott described so sensitively. For many babies the weaning process may feel like something frightening and depriving;

something known and good is being taken away and being replaced by something strange and difficult and unpleasant. The sweet milk (and it is remarkable just how sweet breast milk is; cows' milk has sugar added to it as part of the process of modifying it for babies) is replaced by an alien texture and taste.

It seems likely that these early feeding experiences lead to various sorts of food misuse. One is the feeling of not being able to rely on there being food again — the need to eat to satiety now because the opportunity will not come again. An echo of weaning, perhaps, lies in the preference of many food misusers for foods that are sweet and easy to eat, requiring little chewing. Could this be why fast food chains such as MacDonalds are so successful and why so many people like ice cream and soft drinks? Maybe a lot of us learned to doubt and misunderstand our feelings of hunger. Probably most of us did not have enough of that early experience of breast/bottle feeding and we find culturally approved ways of making up for ourselves for the nasty shock of it being brought to an end so soon.

There is a great deal more to eating disorders than the attempt to reverse or recreate early feeding experience, but the central importance of that experience in our infant lives makes it worth considering and investigating. If you want to think about your misuse of food, it might be worth trying to explore that subject by talking to those who knew you as a baby. Perhaps you can learn something about the roots of your present difficulties in that early history.

FOOD AS PART OF AN EARLY POWER STRUGGLE

However, the meaning of food and eating does not only derive from our infant experience. We have a whole lifetime of personal meanings to add to those beginnings.

The next in chronological order, and one that may well be within reach of conscious memory for some of us, is the battle that is often conducted over food with toddlers and young children. We have all heard adults say with mingled amounts of pride, despair and annoyance about young children, 'Oh, she's got a mind of her own.' Children naturally develop the capacity to want, whether it is the rattle held out to them in earliest infancy or the more sophisticated playthings and experiences of later childhood. In this wanting lies the kernel of our capacity to grow into adults who will be able to make good choices for ourselves and for our lives. Parents often find this wanting hard to deal with anyway, and can feel challenged by a child's capacity to want differently from its parents. It is difficult, and probably impossible, to get right the balance between allowing children freedom to choose and appropriately limiting their choices, especially as the territory is always moving anyway. It is easy to offer a 2-year-old the choice between milk and juice, but what about the 5-year-old who wants coffee or the 7-year-old who wants beer?

Unfortunately it is often food which is chosen as the battleground on which the child's struggle for separation and independence is worked out. And these issues are complicated by the meanings of food and feeding as loving and caring that were referred to in connection with infant feeding. Parents, especially mothers, can have too much invested in getting their child to eat everything up. Not eating can too easily be seen as rejection of what has been offered and therefore of the one who offers it. I remember reading advice to mothers not to take too much time or trouble over preparing darling little meals for tiny children. If the child spits out what you have taken hours to make, you are much more likely to be upset than if it took you ten minutes and/or (perish the thought) you opened a packet or a tin. It seems an appropriate acknowledgement of the fact that it's easy for mothers to feel rejected and upset over children's eating behaviour, and easy to be emotionally over-invested in whether the little one eats her egg.

In this sense of rejection lie the roots of the anger and the power struggle that so frequently follow a child's refusal of food. Of course parents can justify anger by reference to what they think are the child's needs, yet it is widely known and understood that there is a time in the lives of young children when their need for food diminishes sharply. We also know because we have read it a hundred times that if a child is normal in every other way and full of energy, then however little food she gets it is enough. This truth can be hard to hang on to when all your child will eat is peanut butter sandwiches, but it is sometimes reassuring.

Despite this we nevertheless try and force children to eat. Why? Perhaps it has something to do with the unpalatable fact that as parents it is our function to become unnecessary. In the first intimation of the fact that our child is capable of not wanting what we want is the distant trumpet call that sounds the end of our usefulness in that role. Our violence in reinforcing our will is the measure of how hard it is for us to endure that hard fact.

Often people write as though the difficulties over children's eating behaviour were only to do with the child. It is also very much to do with the parent. An authority on psychological matters was writing about how children have to learn to deal with frustration. He (it was a man) suggested that it was appropriate to make children finish food and to eat food they did not like in order to accustom them to frustration. This quite remarkably stupid advice reveals an author apparently unaware of the many, many necessary frustrations in a child's everyday life. To advocate adding food to the list not only sets the stage for endless battles, but lays the foundations for trouble in the future.

Two adults, Gordon and Hilda, both in their fifties, were discussing their experience with food as children. Hilda told how as a child she was required to eat everything put in front of her, whether she liked it or not, and whether she was hungry or not. If she would not eat it she was given nothing else to eat and at each meal what she had not previously eaten was put in front of her until she did. Such brutal and humiliating ways of dealing with children are perhaps not quite as common these days. Gordon then told how he was allowed to eat what he wanted. At one time for a while he ate nothing but bananas and orange juice. At this point in the story Hilda, his wife, interrupted to say how very spoiled and indulged he had been as a child. The interesting thing is that one of these adults is what is called a 'picky eater' and dislikes a great many foods. The other is a curious and adventurous eater and will try anything. I will leave you to work out which is which.

Once the power struggle is located in food, then both parties are likely to play the game with great enthusiasm and persistence. That is bad enough in itself, but there is worse to follow. It seems that often the struggle we carried on in reality as small children with our parents, we continue as grown people in our heads. We install the parent figure inside us. We internalise her (him, them) and we continue to respond to this internal parent as we responded, or wanted to respond, to the real parent.

Isobel came from a family where food was in short supply. This was not because there was any lack of money but because Isobel's mother believed in strictly limiting portions of food. She always bought the absolute minimum quantities of everything and never kept any supplies in the cupboard. Each day's food was bought a day at a time and there were no extras to allow for unexpected changes or snacks. So there were never any biscuits or any 'instant food' for peckish moments.

Isobel had coped with this mean and depriving household as best she could — because, of course, what went with it was a mother who felt that her emotional resources were in as short supply as the food and who found it impossible to respond with generosity to the emotional hunger of her family. As a child Isobel found substitute mothers in her teachers and the families of her friends and then from her mid-teens in sexual relationships with boys considerably older than herself from whom she could get some 'mothering'. This system broke down when she left her home town to go to college. There she began to eat voraciously, eating to fill the void of unlovedness, but also to defy the mother who practised such rigid portion control. To eat a whole packet of biscuits became an act of hatred and revenge against the mother who now in reality was quite unable to limit Isobel's consumption.

WOMEN AND FOOD — THE DILEMMA

This account of Isobel and her mother makes clear another aspect of food use which is particularly difficult for women. This is that mothers (girlfriends, wives, sisters) are often the ones who do the preparing of food, the shopping and cooking, but are also the ones required to limit their food intake. Feminists have made us aware of the cultural requirement for women to be thin. As they have pointed out, virtually all women's magazines will contain sections on food restriction for women ('The Three Day Diet'; 'Get your Body Ready for the Beach', etc.). Side by side with these instructions will be others urging them to feed their families ('Hearty Puddings for your Family'; 'Scrumptious Casseroles for Hungry Males', etc.). The apparent requirement is that we starve ourselves while urging others to eat ('Go on, eat it up; it'll do you good.').

This complex message about how to deal with food in relation to our families is paralleled by what is often understood by women as the demand to take care of everyone else and not to take care of themselves. Women are to be generous with others emotionally, take care of their needs and wants, but ignore their own needs. This painful dynamic — and the transmission of it from mother to daughter — has been described by Susie Orbach and others. These cultural messages make it extremely hard for women to know whether they are allowed to eat, or certainly what and how much. Many of the women I talked to said they had an index in their heads of forbidden foods — forbidden, that is, to them, but not to others. Food is made to do the work of all kinds of complicated feelings about loving and not loving.

THE ROLE OF FOOD IN THE FAMILY

This brings us to another dimension of our experience of food and eating. We have been talking so far about the relationship between mother (or primary caregiver) and child in relation to food. Although that is an extremely important dimension of our experience, it is only part of it. There is the whole issue of the meaning of food in our family. What were food and mealtimes used for in our households?

The Jardine family were noisy, boisterous and numerous. Their mealtimes were times of exuberant conversation during which they competed with one another for conversational space. They kept open house and the children's friends frequently came and joined in these high-spirited occasions. Kate, their mother, was an exceptionally good cook and produced, apparently without undue effort, large quantities of good food. Leonard, their father, was a supportive and appreciative husband who frequently thanked his wife for the excellent food that all of them had just enjoyed. For the Jardine mealtimes were joyful opportunities for celebration. This is not to say that they did not have their sorrows or their quarrels, but mealtimes were often happy occasions.

Interestingly enough the Jardines were all slightly overweight, as if the pleasure of eating and mealtimes was too good to resist, but none of them appeared to mind. Perhaps this can support what I am trying to say about the use of food. If you use food to celebrate as the Jardines did and in the process get rather plump, that is only an issue if it makes you unhappy. If you enjoy the way you use food, there is no problem. This is where I agree with the feminist writers who have urged women to let themselves find out what size and shape they want to be, regardless of what the advertising industry holds up for admiration.

The Knight family, on the other hand, had dismal and frightening mealtimes. The father of the family, Malcolm, was a violent and evil-tempered man who terrorised his wife Nora and their children. Mealtimes were the times when he chose to pick on his family for their table manners, their clothes, what they said or the way they said it, the expression on their faces, anything or nothing. Many, many mealtimes ended with violent rages from Malcolm and tears from one or other of the family. The daughter of the family, Olivia, dealt with this situation by spending as much time as possible away from home. When she had to be part of the family she would often eat very quickly, as did her brother, apparently in an attempt to bring the meal to an end as soon as possible. Sometimes, however, the tension made it hard for her to eat and she would have times of eating very little.

As an adult Olivia found herself repeating exactly this pattern. Tension, distress, upset would provoke either a lot of rapid and rather uncontrolled eating or an anorexic episode during which she would eat very little. It was exceedingly difficult for her to establish a regular, normal pattern of eating, and her weight fluctuated accordingly.

Patrick was brought up by his elderly grandparents. They were devoted to him but continued a pattern of existence that had been established for years and into which, as a late and unexpected arrival on the scene, he was never really integrated. Throughout his schooldays he ate alone. He would come home from school in the middle of the day or after school and would be given his meal to eat alone. There would be nothing wrong with the food but Patrick always found it difficult to concentrate on eating it. He said that he always felt as if he wanted to be out playing with his friends. His grandmother did not keep him company while he ate; it was an occasion without any kind of emotional attraction. Patrick found it extremely difficult to force himself to eat when he moved away from home. His weight was well below normal and he experienced a continual revulsion from food. However, when he began to form close relationships and to discover the pleasure of shared meals he began to be alive to how he had been continuing his family tradition with his solitary reluctant eating.

Roberta lived alone with her mother who was a nurse and worked on night shift. She had a close and even rather clinging relationship with her mother and very few friends, so that she was accustomed to spending her evenings at home. When she came in her mother had already left for work so Roberta made her own supper and ate it in front of the television. She was lonely and hungry for her mother, but she disguised these facts from herself by turning on the television and spending the evening comforting herself with food. As she said, 'I just sit in front of the television and never notice how much I'm putting in my mouth.'

Mr and Mrs Simpson, an elderly couple, lived a life that was very unstimulating and boring. They were disappointed in life generally, which seemed to them to have been a series of hazards and crises only narrowly avoided. They saw the world outside their front door as full of danger, so they felt safer at home, living a limited but reliable routine. In this routine food assumed great importance: the planning, shopping, cooking, eating and clearing up occupied a large part of the day and their energies. This process had been going on for many years so that Mrs Simpson had steadily eaten herself to a mountainous size. In order to control the resulting hypertension, heart disease and numerous other side effects of her weight, she took large quantities of drugs which in turn produced unpleasant side effects of their own. But to the doctor's suggestion that she lose weight she responded only that she was too old, that it didn't matter, and that in any case she ate very little. 'After all,' she remarked to her husband, 'what else is there to live for?'

Mealtimes serve very different purposes in different households and form part of our experience of food. None of these examples may exactly match your own experience, but perhaps thinking about them will enable you to identify what mealtimes were for you in your family and whether you are continuing, or want to continue, that pattern and tradition.

However, food also has a meaning in families over and

above the meaning of mealtimes. Deprivation of food, for example, is commonly used as a punishment. It can be an experience which lasts a lifetime. A woman in her fifties told me over and over again the story of the supper party held by her parents to which the children of the family were allowed to come. She as the youngest child was indulged when she began to entertain the company, but her tricks went on too long, her charm ceased to amuse and her entertainment ended in her being sent to bed without any supper. At a distance of fifty years that punishment still had power to sting.

A much younger woman, Antonia, had considerably harsher treatment to deal with. Her mother had died when she was only 8 years old and her father was emotionally very ill-equipped to take care of four small children, of whom Antonia was the eldest. His methods of dealing with them were extremely unpleasant. Starvation was one of them. For trivial (or not so trivial) offences Antonia would be locked in her room for days. Only her father's wealth and position in the community protected him from prosecution for ill-treatment of his children. Antonia was unable to deal with food in a relaxed way. As a child she had stolen food, both at home where it was kept under lock and key, and from shops. A severe but short-lived anorexic few months at the age of 16 and 17 were followed by several years of very troubled eating behaviour. For a while things would be all right and then Antonia would be tormented by the urge to binge.

Perhaps more commonly than deprivation of food being used as a punishment, food can be used as a comfort. Many mothers comfort their children when they fall down with a sweet. Dentists have mostly turned to comforting their young patients with balloons rather than sweets, but doctors still hand out a sweet or a lollipop after an injection. Perhaps it is no wonder that we even have a phrase 'comfort eating' to describe this kind of consolation. And the 'comfort' for grown people is not so much for physical hurts as for emotional pain, not so much for hurt knees as for hurt feelings.

And of course food is used as a reward and as a bribe. Sometimes when I have worked with people with eating disorders we have together devised reward systems to help them achieve changes in their eating behaviour. One of the great difficulties has been for these clients to find rewards for themselves which were *not* food. This is the cluster of feelings so accurately identified in the advertisement for cream cakes. 'Naughty but nice'. We are so thoroughly caught up in this way of seeing food that we give it all kinds of meanings. Two women were chatting at a social occasion when they were offered pieces of 'millionaire's shortbread', shortbread covered with toffee and then with chocolate. One woman refused it on the grounds that it was immoral. Shortbread, she said, should not be covered with all that stuff. It was bad enough on its own but with topping like that it was morally offensive. Her companion, taking a piece, said that it was impossible for a biscuit to have moral value. A biscuit could not be good or bad. Can it?

The reward/bribe system works at a number of levels in our society. Business circles use it a great deal. Directors' dining rooms, expense account lunches and dinners, Christmas parties for the staff: these are all part of it. In fact, eating and food have become so important in our society that they confer status and importance. And of course where food is plentiful, as it is in our society, then all kinds of subtle meanings become attached to what is eaten when. We are none of us immune to all of this. The immense number of opportunities to eat, the endless attempts to titillate our jaded palates with new combinations or new ideas all combine to push us further and further away from the capacity to listen to our bodies' needs and supply them appropriately.

Take, for example, the confectionery industry's attempts to get us to use their products. They present us with the most extravagant rewards and associations to putting into our bodies something which has no nutritional value, indeed something which may well rob our bodies of nutrients. It is indicated to us that we will be socially and sexually successful. We will be beautiful. We will be young. We will be rich and leisured. Many of us are not able to resist these blandishments. That is what is intended and hoped for.

CURRENT PATTERNS OF EATING

It is now more than 40 years since the end of the Second World War, but in our (Western European) society there are still large numbers of people who remember rationing. It is now a nutritionist's commonplace to say that rationing was the best thing that ever happened to Britain because it obliged people to eat in a relatively healthy way. It was, however, not a matter of choice. As anyone will tell you who remembers those times, nobody got fat during rationing. There was a strict limit on calorie intake imposed by scarcity.

If we think about the time before the Second World War we are talking about times before the advent of the Welfare State, before the increased prosperity that we enjoy now, and when there was widespread poverty and acute hunger. There were great inequalities in society, and certainly not everyone went hungry or anything like it, but food was not as plentiful in the sense of being within the financial reach of all.

It is, then, only in the last thirty years or so that our society has been as glutted with food as it is now, and that consequently the pressures to eat have become as enormous as they are. Take a couple of small examples. Thirty years ago it was uncommon to see people eating and drinking on the streets and in public places. Now it is commonplace. Similarly, not so long ago eating between meals, even if it was a common enough activity, was thought to be a bad idea. Now for increasing numbers of people there are no established mealtimes and changes in the food industry have eroded established patterns of what to eat. The phenomenon known as 'grazing' is upon us where it is normal to eat all day long in an unstructured way and without much reference to time of day. The old certainties of how much of what to eat when are disappearing. For those of us whose inner psychological certainty about food has been damaged, the trackless territory of contemporary eating behaviour creates tremendous problems. Interestingly enough, programmes for recovering food misusers often include a requirement to eat in a thoroughly conventional way at fixed mealtimes, so that in one dimension at least there is some guidance.

Some Western European countries — perhaps France, Spain, Italy, maybe others — seem to the casual observer at least to have suffered less disintegration in family structures than Britain or the USA. In these countries meals seem a much more important family occasion and to have retained formal and ritual value. This may, perhaps, help those who otherwise might lose their bearings completely about food and hunger.

Quite apart from the personal and inner difficulties with food, society as a whole has not adapted well to the constant availability and abundance of food. So far as I know, no society has. North America has had to deal with the situation longer than Western Europe; the difficulties this created started earlier and chart a path that it looks as if we are following.

However, it could only be in a society in which food was so immensely important that eating disorders would make sense. This is very obviously the case with anorexia. To put it crudely: if you are anorexic in a society in which many people are underfed then you are not so remarkable, but to starve in a society of overfed people is something very different. This is equally true of obesity. In a society where food is in short supply, then to be fat is a signal of the power to choose to eat when that power is not general. It therefore conveys wealth or status within the society. Where we all have the opportunity to overeat, the fact that only some take it gives that gesture emotional meaning and significance. If, even more strangely, people eat and then get rid of the food so that it cannot nourish them, they make an even more violent statement.

This chapter has shown how our personal experience and the society in which we live supply us with a context for our eating behaviour. This experience does not necessarily turn us into food misusers, but it does give us a language, a way of behaving, if we get to the point of feeling that we have to use it. It gives us weapons, ammunition of a certain kind, if we need to take them up. What I now want to go on to explore is what reasons there might be for us taking up these very powerful weapons.

SECTION TWO

3
EATING DISORDERS AS A RESPONSE TO CRISIS

This [behaviour in crisis] was a temporary hitch in a reasonably well-managed life.

Ellen Noonan, *Counselling Young People*

In the first chapter of this section we looked at the emotional meaning of the use of food, food misuse. Let us now consider it as a response to crisis. Take this very mild and very common example: a young woman goes out to a party or for a meal. She eats far more than she wants to and comes home feeling angry that she has not exerted more self-control. She asks herself why she did it and produces a range of answers that sound possible, but not convincing: she had to eat not to offend her hostess; she was just greedy and lost control; she didn't notice that she was eating too much; she particularly liked the food and couldn't resist eating too much. But if we explore a little more carefully what this young woman was feeling before she went to the party we discover that there was a mixture of feelings about it, not all of which were very easy to deal with. Yes, she was looking forward to it, but she also felt anxious about it. Who would she meet? What would people think of the way she looked or danced? Perhaps she also felt sexually excited and couldn't feel very contented or relaxed with that feeling. Perhaps with a part of her she didn't want to go to the party at all, felt resentful and angry because she would have preferred to do something else.

There could be any number of feelings associated with a social event of this kind and feelings that are difficult for one person will be pleasurable for another. The point is that for some women one way of dealing with those difficult feelings is to smother them with food. Now this may be the way some women have developed of dealing with difficult feelings. In this chapter, however, I'm suggesting that it can be the way some women respond to crisis, to a particular situation, that for them feels particularly difficult.

There is, of course, no good reason why a woman should abandon this way of coping if it causes her no pain. After all, if she occasionally eats too much or doesn't eat enough as a way of dealing with a crisis, no great harm has been done. We all need some defences and that one may be as good as any. However, some women don't like the way they use food, are bothered by it, don't understand it, and would like to change, and it is to them that this is directed.

We use our emergency ways of coping when we feel most under stress or threat. One of the commonest and most obvious of these situations is when a girl leaves home for the first time. Very often this move to college or to her own place is accompanied by a quite considerable weight gain or loss. This is such a frequent occurrence that there is a whole series of common sense reasons that are produced to explain it: the food in the hostel is stodgy; she doesn't like the food they give her; she's eating too much fast food instead of cooking for herself; she's not eating a balanced diet; she doesn't know how to cook properly; the cooking facilities aren't very good; she has to share the kitchen with so many other people; she's a vegetarian and the hostel gives her such boring vegetarian food — and so on.

Yet it seems that for many young people, leaving home for the first time is an especially difficult moment in their lives. It doesn't help that it is probably something they wanted to do with a sizeable chunk of themselves, that they were thoroughly fed up with living at home and very conscious of its problems and disadvantages. They expected to be able to make a painless transition into independent living and very probably other people expected it of them too: 'You'll be looking forward to getting a place of your own ... I expect you're looking forward to doing your own thing ... You'll be glad to get away to college.' Of course, for many there are these feelings, but they are not as simple and unmixed as other people seem to expect, or as they expect of themselves.

What is being referred to here is the ordinary anxiety about transition from being an adolescent living at home to being a young adult establishing her own independence. It does not refer to the much more serious difficulties to be discussed later of those eating disorders that are the effect of serious and long-standing problems in making the transition from child to adolescent to adult. However, because these more short-lived difficulties are not so serious, it does not mean that they are not painful.

FIONA'S STORY

Fiona got herself a place at a college in London a long way from her family home. Her family lived in a quiet, remote part of the country and there lived a quiet, rather old-fashioned and conservative life. Fiona was herself a rather quiet, conservative, old-fashioned girl. However, she obviously, with part of herself at least, wanted something more exciting or she would never have contemplated so radical a move. The reality of living and going to college in London was horrifying to her. She was appalled by the way her fellow students spoke and behaved. She was shocked by their bad language and their sexually explicit conversations. She was threatened by their active sexuality, by the self-confidence, as she saw it, the pushiness, of some of the students. She felt there was almost no one like her and her obvious disapproval and contempt for her fellow students certainly did not help her to make friends. She could survive in an alienated kind of way while she was actually at college, but when she went home she fell apart. And the band-aid that she chose to cover her wounds with was food. Evening after evening she would sit on her own in the deserted kitchen of the hostel eating bread and butter, for her the symbolic food of childhood and of home. By half-term she had gained a stone in weight and lost a ton in confidence and self-esteem. She suffered worst from agonies of home-sickness and it was this feeling in particular that she tried to anaesthetise with food. With dogged courage she stuck out most of the first year of her course. It was only when she began to accept that it was no disgrace to be homesick that she could allow herself to consider other courses and other colleges nearer home.

There was nothing wrong with Fiona's development as an adolescent, but she had made a change that was more than she was ready for at the time. When she could feel that she need not be ashamed of her feelings, she did not need to try to obliterate them with bread and butter but instead could begin to make plans that were more appropriate to her temperament and her emotional development.

ALISTAIR'S STORY

A young man, Alistair, came to college in London from a background not unlike Fiona's: quiet, conservative and provincial. He, however, was bursting to get away and longing to sample what London had to offer. Almost immediately, however, he began to lose weight so rapidly and to such an extent that he looked for some help. What emerged was a story of an extremely capable and energetic young man who at the same time was deeply resentful that now he was no longer living at home there was no one to look after him and he had to look after himself. At a practical level the adult part of Alistair was more than capable of doing this, but the child part wanted a mother to take care of him, particularly to cook for him. When there was no one, the hurt and angry child part of him responded by not eating. Now on top of this dynamic there was a whole layer of apparent reasons why Alistair hadn't been eating: there wasn't time to shop or cook; his grant was late so he had no money; he didn't know how or what to cook and so on. Nevertheless, although there was truth in all of this, the guts of the situation was that Alistair wasn't eating because he was so upset and angry about leaving home (and what home meant — having his meals provided for him). When he could accept that there was a bit of him that felt like that, and that his grief and upset at leaving home was usual and normal, then he could begin to enjoy his independence and take pleasure in becoming a very competent cook.

TIME TO MOURN

In both of these situations there had been some emotional work left undone, very possibly emotional work for which there was no encouragement or opportunity for these two people. And that emotional work is the work of grieving. Most of us think about our lives as progress (at least to middle age) towards something better. The advantages of being older and more grown up than in fact we are appear constantly before our eyes. This applies not only to the natural urge for physical mastery and maturity — co-ordination, physical strength, height, weight — but also in adolescents to social mastery. The freedoms to smoke, drink, stay up late, go out without adults, have sexual experience, see adult films, earn more money: these are very seductively displayed and make it difficult some-times for us to allow ourselves to be the age we are emotionally and chronologically. One effect of this, then, is that it is hard to mourn for the pleasures of the part of our life that we are leaving behind. Peter Pan gets very little sympathy these days, yet I suspect there are few of us who entered puberty and adolescence without a pang for what we were leaving behind.

There is a similar story to be told at the point of transition from adolescence to young adulthood. To express sadness at leaving home — sadness that a whole part of our life with our parents is over — is not always very easy. The cultural climate does not encourage it. But nevertheless the evidence is that such natural mourning is not an optional extra but a necessary and desirable part of our capacity to take up the challenges of the next stage of our development.

FOOD AND RELATIONSHIPS

Another area of crisis is that of relationships. It is very common for women who use food in crisis to binge or starve when relationships go wrong — especially love relationships. Again it is the ordinary ups and downs that are part of the process of looking for a long-term partner that are being talked about here, not the more serious eating disorders (to be discussed later) where those who find it exceedingly difficult to form relationships at all may use eating disorders as a holding pattern to keep the whole issue at a distance. However, the 'ordinariness' of such crises in no way diminishes their capacity to cause a lot of pain.

Take, for example, the story of Iris, a lively, clever, funny, popular girl who lived an extremely busy, active social life. One of the reasons she was so popular was that she was always good-tempered, always smiling. When she split up with her boyfriends, she didn't feel it bothered her. She got a bit upset, that was all: easy come, easy go. Her sadness soon passed and she was her old self again.

But underneath this jolly coping self was a girl who dealt with the crises with the men in her life by eating. This fact she kept secret from herself for a long time, although she was upset by her inability to keep her weight down. She did not know in any sort of conscious way what she was doing. Anyway, this system had worked not badly for about three years, so why should she know? But one autumn she broke up with a boy whom she had been very fond of. Her weight increased. She began not to cope at work. She started taking a lot of time off and became depressed. Depression was something new in her life. She had, as far as she could remember, never felt so miserable before. It was sufficiently alarming for her to seek help, particularly because, as she said, nothing was wrong in her life. She didn't know what she was depressed about. So far as she was concerned it had just happened to her.

Gradually, as she began to try to remember when she got depressed and what had been happening in her life at that time, it became obvious to her that she had been upset by the break-up with her boyfriend. But that was a puzzle to her because she didn't get upset about boyfriends. Then, without recognising the connection, Iris began to talk about the real problem in her life: her failure to control her weight and eating. Soon she began to see the connection. Maybe she didn't consciously get upset, but certainly something was hurting inside when she stuffed herself with food. Then we began to talk about her family and how they dealt with crisis. The answer was that they didn't. No one was allowed to get upset, particularly not Iris. Her mother insisted that Iris always presented a smiling face and had been known to hang up on her if her telephone calls were not sufficiently up-beat.

In fact, Iris's problems with food were quite an ingenious way of dealing with distress that she had never learned to express more openly. However, it was a system that had not proved strong enough to cope with a really painful loss. Her pain had emerged as depression. How was she going to do it differently?

There were lots of things going for Iris. One was that, although she had a family and a mother who had difficult-ies in dealing with crisis, she was fortunate that her childhood had nevertheless had lots of good things about it. She was a much-loved and cared for child. So she was not as a young woman in crisis trying to deal with a not very good beginning, as so many of those to be described in this book have had to do. If you like, all she needed was to be helped to find a way to respond more directly to her relationships with men. Secondly, she badly wanted to be rid of her problems with food. She wanted to lose weight and become as beautiful as undoubtedly she would be. She was tired of fighting herself about food all the time. So she was well-motivated to try a different way of doing it. Thirdly, although she was scared of feeling her pain, she was not very, very scared. Somewhere inside her there was a very strong, capable person (carefully nurtured by her parents) who was tough enough to survive a lot.

When we had reached this point in our discussions, I didn't see Iris for several weeks. When she came back she told me this story. She had been going on a trip with a boy who was a close friend. They were looking for the place they wanted to visit, but by mistake took a wrong turning in the car. The anxiety and frustration of the situation made Iris cry, and once started she found it hard to stop. Her friend asked her how he could help and she told him that she wanted him to take her home to his flat. This he did and he stayed with her, taking care of her. She cried for almost three days, over all the things she had not cried about for three years. She said that during those three days she had realised what a lot she had not felt and how much feeling there was to do. She said that it had been awful and terrible, but in a positive kind of way, and that she had felt incredibly much better since.

One of the remarkable things about this story is how, once given permission, Iris knew exactly what she needed to do. What's more, she could find the time and the occasion, the safe person and the safe place. Without consciously planning it, she had supplied herself with a very good opportunity to catch up on her backlog of emotional work.

Undoubtedly this is not the end of the story. Human beings don't change as fast as that. However, there has been a remarkable shift in Iris's ability to express her feelings directly. With support and encouragement there is a good chance of a lasting change. At the same time Iris's eating disorder has shrunk from being a monster to being a tendency that she knows about. When Iris wants to over-eat these days, she is beginning to be able to stop and ask herself the question: 'What's upsetting me today?'

Exactly the same mechanism at work with Iris is acted

out with people whose tendency is to anorexia rather than to compulsive eating. When things go badly in their intimate relationships, they starve themselves. This is not to be confused with the loss of appetite that goes with grief and mourning. The anorexia is *instead* of grief and mourning; it actually prevents any grieving and mourning. Grieving and mourning is an acknowledgement of emotional needs, hungers, dependencies, a process by which it is possible to come to terms with loss. It is that pain of need and loss that not eating is intended to abolish.

DEALING WITH ANGER

A third category of crisis to which women respond with food misuse is anger. It may seem a strange idea that anger is itself a crisis, but many women have no idea what to do with their hatred and rage, except to express it in ways that hurt themselves. On the face of it, lots and lots of women with minor eating disorders are unhappy, miserable, powerless. When women talk to me about themselves they often tell me a terrible story in which, however, no anger or outrage is expressed at all. But sometimes I know that there is rage because I feel it myself physically in my chest. Suddenly I will feel furiously angry on this woman's behalf and want to fight for her against all the injustices she has suffered. That isn't my anger (although I have plenty of my own). It's her anger that I'm feeling, and I'm feeling it because she can't bear to feel it. This is the fury that is expressed in the violence of eating disorders. There is nothing gentle about them; they are not pleasant or nice. They are extremely powerful. Think about the ferocious biting, gulping, chewing, swallowing of a binge; think about the hatred that is expressed in refusing to eat. Many people with eating disorders can easily express their hatred and contempt for themselves; but to suggest that those feelings are really meant for someone else: 'No, no: certainly not. Love and peace, sister'.

So when a woman with a tendency to express her feelings by her eating behaviour is made angry, her anger goes underground and reappears as an attack on herself via food. The process is so customary that it is invisible. She literally swallows her anger. Think of this scenario, which I hear repeatedly. A dance student is in class and is reprimanded for something she is not doing correctly. She feels the comment is harsh or unjust and she struggles to control her tears and to stay in the class. Often in this situation the student will cry or leave the class. She then goes and buys herself chocolate and eats it quickly. Maybe she then goes into another shop and does the same. As soon as she has done, maybe even while she's eating the chocolate bar, she's filled with violent rage and hatred of *herself.* So it seems. She doesn't see the connection between what happened in class and her eating behaviour. If she goes home to make herself sick or take laxatives, she doesn't feel that as rage with her teacher either. She is totally convinced that she is not an angry person. She feels that she is pathetic and a victim.

When my clients start to feel angry, I feel like standing on the table and cheering, because I know that that is the beginning of the end for the eating disorder. Women don't need the feminists to remind them of the cultural embargo on women's anger, but they do badly need to learn that they can be angry without the sky falling on their heads. Think about what you do when you get angry. Do you even know? And what happened when you got angry when you were growing up? Were you allowed to be angry? Were you ever angry?

Of course, it's not as easy as that. Women don't just need permission to be angry, although that helps. (One girl came to see me, her face blazing with triumph, 'I got angry! I got angry!'). Women are also afraid of what their anger will do; they are afraid of its power. Sometimes it is necessary to find a safe person, and a safe place in which to be angry. One woman I worked with went around being nice to everyone. She thought that if she wasn't nice all the time, then no one would like her. Once she got used to me and able to believe that I would stick with her anyway, she used to practise being angry. It wasn't fun for either of us, and I used to cringe when she slammed the door behind her, but it was very, very necessary. It made her feel much better and loosened the grip of her eating disorder.

EATING YOUR WORRIES AWAY

Lastly there are eating disorders which arise as a response to 'worry'. If a woman puts on weight or loses it, there's a common or garden, everyday, kind of explanation often right at hand, 'Oh, she's been worried.' However a more accurate description might be, 'She was trying not to worry.' Everyone has lots of things to worry about — money, exams, relationships, work, families. Many people lead complicated, successful lives, trying to respond to all sorts of demands. Often a solution to all this pressure is to try to obliterate the worry with food or starvation, rather than to think about what is causing the worry.

There is, that is to say, a positive and creative form of worrying, a necessary and desirable form of worrying — 'worry work'. Of course it is possible to worry in a way that prevents any emotional work being done. We can revolve endlessly and pointlessly in our heads about the things that bother us. This is the kind of worrying that gets us nowhere — the worrying whether the back door is locked, the worry whether the house is tidy enough, the worry about money and paying the bills. We can worry about them without ever really tackling the subject of our worries. But there is another form of worry that is valuable and necessary. If I'm lying in bed worrying whether the back door is locked, then I should get out of bed and look. That kind of worry — of appropriate concern — pushes us into doing what we actually need to do. It is this sort of creative worrying that we can fail to do if we use food to prevent it.

Take a common enough situation — a young woman is due to take an examination in two days time. She's worried about it, but she doesn't let herself worry creatively. Instead she sits down with her books, a packet of biscuits and a cup of coffee. She's so distracted by the biscuits, their smell and the look of them that she can't concentrate. She feels she shouldn't have one, but she does and then she wants more. She eats them, one by one, feeling so guilty that she can't concentrate. She's worrying, in a pointless kind of way, about her examination, but she's also using food to stop herself worrying. If she worked at her worry she would know she needs to revise one set of notes tonight and another set tomorrow night and then she might have a chance of passing her examination. At the moment she thinks she's working but really she's wondering whether she should make herself sick because she's eaten a whole packet of biscuits and if she goes on like this she'll be as fat as a pig.

It can go the other way, of course. A woman is going for an interview and decides that she won't get the job until she's thinner. She's so confused about the difference between 'herself' and her appearance that she is trying to improve her chances of getting the job by being thinner. So then she spends the next ten days worrying about weight and food and size and calories and no time at all thinking about how to present 'herself' at the interview. This is a shame because in order to do well at the interview she needs to spend time to prepare her thoughts and ideas. In fact she needs to work at it, but she doesn't. She stops herself from doing necessary worry work.

This is not by any means an exhaustive list of the crises that people may meet in their lives, but it is enough to illustrate the point. Our eating behaviour may cause us little difficulty except in crisis, and then we can suddenly find ourselves bingeing or starving. If we can permit ourselves to make the link between what is going on in our lives and what we are doing with food, we may not have to resort to such a painful way of coping.

4
ON BEING A WOMAN

It is the thesis of this book that compulsive eating in women is a response to their social position.

Susie Orbach, *Fat is a Feminist Issue*

The associations produced by food, the memories and the history of our experience with food that were discussed in Chapter 2 are, of course, not just the property of women. We all, male and female, have a lifetime of eating to remember. However, eating disorders are, very largely, a women's complaint. Why is that? It has already been suggested that part of the answer may be that women tend to express their distress in ways that hurt themselves rather than turning it out and against other people. However the question has been answered further by feminist writers and this chapter takes a look at some aspects of their understanding of why women are so tormented by issues of size, of food and of eating.

Morag's initial complaint was not that she had difficulties with food but that she was depressed. When she began to talk about her life it didn't seem very surprising: here was a healthy young woman of 20 living a life of such monotony and boredom that she had every right to be depressed. Morag was a student in her second year at university, surrounded on every side by the attractions and stimulus not only of her studies and the student community, but by the cultural and social riches of London. Amid this plenty Morag lived a rigid and undeviating routine. She got up at the same time, ate her meals at the same time, studied at the same place in the same library at the same time every day. Weekends caused her great anxiety because the structure of her life was not so rigidly provided by lectures and tutorials, so that she performed her domestic chores such as doing her laundry and cleaning her room in the student hostel with the undeviating regularity with which she attended classes. A tiny indication that there might be another Morag hidden somewhere beneath this mass of rules and regulations was provided by her membership of a church choir. But even this activity was undertaken with the same relentless regularity as the rest of her life.

Morag was also considerably overweight and dressed in a parody of middle-aged fashion. Probably her dress style was modelled on her mother's but in any case it conveyed a woman whose sense of her own possibilities of being physically attractive was very much damaged. In fact she looked a boring frump. Gradually, as we talked, more details emerged of Morag's way of life and of her sadness and despair. She had some female friends at the chuch she attended, and occasionally went out with them. Similarly she had found another woman at her hostel. The pair of them used to meet each evening at 10 p.m. to drink hot chocolate before bed-time at 10.30. Part of Morag stoutly defended this way of living. She found academic work difficult so she needed lots of time to study — she needed to copy out her lecture notes each day, it was her way of learning. She didn't want to go out in the evenings — it made her too tired the next day. She didn't want to go to parties as crowds of people made her anxious. Besides, sometimes she did go to films with her friends.

But with another part of her Morag was lonely, unhappy and dissatisfied. She was particularly concerned about her weight and size. 'If only' she constantly said, 'if only I was thinner I wouldn't feel so bad. I wouldn't mind going out if I didn't feel as if everyone was looking at me, thinking "God, she's fat".' Gradually she was able to tell me about her struggles with food and how she sometimes spent the weekend in a frenzy of misery.

What was it all about? In time Morag was able to tell me

about her family, and then the picture became a little clearer. Her father was a bully and a drunkard who terrorised his wife and two children. He was capable of violent rages especially if some detail of the domestic arrangements failed to please him. Morag's mother was a drudge in this household, afraid of her husband and abused by him. He had many ways of maintaining his tyranny not least of which had been to deprive his family of money. Morag's mother had focused her energies on trying to protect the girls from him.

Not surprisingly, Morag had been glad to escape from this environment and her diligence at school had enabled her to do so via university. However, once there she hardly knew what to do with herself. She had no experience of socialising because she had always been forbidden by her father to go out at night, or to bring friends home. She did not know how to relax and enjoy herself because in order to survive she had created as a schoolgirl a rigid programme of attending to her homework. The undeviating regime she had created at university was her way of continuing this protective system.

But at the same time in some corner of her head Morag knew that there was more to life than the way she was living it. She was curious about boys, but at the same time very frightened of them. In her first year at university she had been invited to the Freshers' Ball, but in total panic had refused the invitation. Since then, however, these anxieties had been overtaken by a constant anxiety about her size. Over and over again she told me that if only she could get thin, her problems would be over.

In due course Morag began to talk about what she might do once she had her degree. She told me that she thought she would like children, but she added she didn't think she wanted a husband, or even a boyfriend. In fact she had wondered if she could make use of the services of a sperm bank. What was it, I wondered aloud to her, that was so unattractive about living with a man. And then out of Morag's mouth came a torrent of words about how horrible men are: how mean, how selfish, how cruel, how unloving. And for a woman to live with a man, I asked? She was a slave, said Morag, taken advantage of, used, a victim. She was much better off on her own.

Morag did not consciously know that she was describing her parents and the relationship between them. Like most of us she assumed that her experience was how it was for everyone. More than most of us, she had had little opportunity for discovering any different. Unconsciously she was convinced that any relationship with a man would place her in the same situation that her mother had been in. Morag's life might be limited but she was not the exploited slave that her mother had become. Her size, her appearance, her way of life, her preoccupation with food were all a way of protecting herself from her mother's fate. She thought of herself as afraid of men and of their sexual impulses, but she was also afraid of her own sexual feelings because they ran the risk of getting her involved with a man.

When Morag began to realise where her image of the role of women came from she began to be able to think about the possibility that there might be other ways of relating to men than the one she saw her mother engaged in. She could begin to think what sort of relationship she might like. As she became less afraid and more hopeful she began to find her problems with food less compulsive and she began to lose weight.

Perhaps Morag represents an extreme example of a woman's rejection of the role of woman presented to her by society. But even if her experience of what it means to be a woman was particularly unpalatable, it provides, I think, a rather good example of how women will use compulsive eating as a protest against being sexual on those terms and as a preoccupation that enables us to push down our sexual feelings. It is very hard to carry on a relationship if you really are absorbed in what you eat, what shape you are and how much you weigh.

THIN IS BEAUTIFUL?

Let us look at this a little more closely. What it suggests is that there is a 'received', accepted shape for a woman to be if she wants to be viewed as a sexual person. This is an idea which has been developed and explored very widely by the feminist writers. In particular the link between these pressures and eating disorders has been elaborated in Britain by Susie Orbach and what follows in this chapter owes a lot to her work. If these ideas are meaningful to you for understanding your eating behaviour, then you should certainly read her work, especially *Fat is a Feminist Issue*. (You will find details of this and her other books in Chapter 10.)

It is not a particularly new idea that women's shape (or the shape to which women are told they should aspire) is dictated by a force outside women themselves. Hilde Bruch in her work on anorexia named 'fashion' as one of the pressures which urge women towards being thin, and in anorexia gets completely out of hand. Indeed the history of fashion is the history of how different parts of the female body have been emphasised at different times and required to be of a certain size and shape. So, for example, low cut, off-the-shoulder and high-waisted garments have all emphasised the breasts; bustles emphasised the bottom; crinolines emphasised the waist. It is also well known that in the pursuit of fashion women have been willing to do themselves physical harm. The tight, lacing stays to make a woman's waist smaller in the late nineteenth century actually caused distortion of the rib cage:

> 'Put down that tray and come lace me tighter,' said Scarlett irritably. 'And I'll try to eat a little afterwards. If I ate now I couldn't lace tight enough.' . . .
>
> 'Hole onter sumpin' and suck in yo' breaf,' Mammy commanded.
>
> Scarlett obeyed, bracing herself and catching firm hold of one of the bedposts. Mammy pulled and jerked vigorously and, as the tiny circumference of whalebone

girdled waist grew smaller, a proud, fond look came into her eyes. . . .

'Now you come eat, honey, but doan eat too fas'. No use havin' it come right back up agin.'

Scarlett obediently sat down before the tray, wondering if she would be able to get any food into her stomach and still have room to breathe.

Margaret Mitchell, *Gone with the Wind*

Our own age is not much different. How many of us have suffered hurt feet and backache from walking or standing in high heels designed to make our feet look dainty and insubstantial? Everybody knows the expression 'Il faut souffrir pour être belle' — you have to suffer to look beautiful. How it translates more accurately is 'a *woman* has to suffer to be beautiful'.

What feminist writers have done, however, is to draw attention to how these ideas about what shape women should be come from outside us. It is not we individually who decide, for example, that this year it will be trendy to show our knees. Fashion is part of an expectation that women will look the way that society wants them to look. It is true, of course, that in terms of fashion in clothes these changes and requirements are far less absolute than they used to be. In terms of body shape there are continuing changes of emphasis from breasts to waist, to legs, to bottom, but the overriding requirement of these externally imposed visions of women is that they are thin.

Those national models of how to be a woman, the Princess of Wales and the Duchess of York (whom we are encouraged to pretend are just like us when the popular press calls them Di and Fergie) are the subject of endless comment about their weight. Princess Diana became rapidly and visibly thinner after her marriage, and enormous pressure has been exerted on the Duchess of York to get her to lose weight. Evidently it is of supreme importance that these two role models get *thin*.

Think for a moment of the images of women presented to us, and the multitude of means of doing so. The advertising industry depicts women on TV, on billboards, in magazines and in newspapers. By these endless visual images we are shown women whose sexual success, attractiveness, wealth, leisure, beauty, youth are all associated with being thin — and of course with whatever product is being promoted.

Now there are very few people who do not wish to be sexually successful, etc, etc. In whatever way they would define those states for themselves, women seem to have bought the message that to achieve these goals they have to be thin. In pursuit of thinness, we spend amazing amounts of money on products which are sold on the basis that they will help keep us thin. Yoghurt, for example, whatever its other merits and food value, is sold very often as a 'slimming food'. Evidently we have been so beguiled by this notion that we need to be told that 'slimming foods' will only aid weight loss as part of a calorie controlled diet. Few women do their food shopping without at the same time thinking of what will or will not keep them thin.

Yet considering all the money and pressure from inside and out, not to mention the time, concern and worry, we seem to make an extraordinarily poor job of keeping thin. It is not necessary to see the actuarial statistics of life assurance companies to know that large numbers of women (and men) are carrying considerably more weight than their frames can manage comfortably, let alone more than the advertising industry decrees. What is more, if we do succeed in getting rid of the extra weight, what do we do but put it straight back on again? Various studies all point to the same conclusion — that virtually all weight lost is regained within two years. In *The Rotation Diet*, the author, Martin Karahn (Bantam 1987), compares the weight loss success story of his institute in St Louis, Missouri, with that of other groups. In comparisons given to prove the success of the institute's own methods, he indicates that in some weight loss programmes the weight gain after the end of the programme was more rapid than the weight loss during it.

The failure to achieve or maintain weight loss is, of

course, put down to lack of persistence, lack of will power, lack of moral fibre, and so on. What feminists have done is to turn this on its head and say that maybe women *don't* want to be thin, that maybe their continuing failure with diets and weight loss, and the way they maintain their fat with compulsive eating, is in some way intentional. Maybe fat serves a purpose for women. And maybe that purpose is to protest against the way women's bodies are objectified and abused, and to protest against the powerless role in society to which women have been relegated.

WOMEN'S POSITION IN SOCIETY

This is not the place to demonstrate point by point the oppression of women, but it is worth just outlining some of the arguments that have been put forward showing how women's place in society is disadvantaged. The economic arguments show first of all that the vast majority of the work that women do in home-making and childcare is unpaid. Since we live in a society where work is valued according to how it is rewarded financially, women's work has come to be regarded as valueless often by the women themselves ('I'm just a housewife') as well as by those around them. Yet whenever the real cost of housekeeping and childcare has to be paid on the open market (housekeepers, nannies, cleaners), the cost of paying for the number of hours a woman works at these tasks is enormous. Secondly when women do work in the open market, their work is less well rewarded, even where they do the equivalent work to men. They do those jobs that have the least status, the fewest prospects of promotion. Proportionately they have far fewer senior positions. They earn less, they inherit less, and therefore in financial terms they control much less. Many, many women have no financial independence from their husbands at all.

The social arguments demonstrate how much of this financial impotence comes about. Women are less well educated, get fewer years of schooling, less training, attend higher and further education in smaller proportions than men, go on to advanced study in smaller numbers. None of this seems to be related to ability or to perceived potential, but to social expectation. There is a wide expectation that after a year or two's work, usually unrelated to a career structure, women will marry and start a family. Their participation in the work world thereafter is anticipated to be part-time and again unrelated to a career structure.

Now it is undeniable that the women's movement has achieved some remarkable changes of attitude and that these inequalities are being eroded. For example, in the mid-sixties roughly one-third of university places in Britain went to women, two-thirds to men. In the mid-eighties almost half go to women. Again, it is still true that women work part time but it is also true that employers are increasingly willing to adapt conditions to women's needs, for instance with regard to holidays and hours. However, there are internalised attitudes in both men and women that prolong oppression and are much harder to erode in either sex.

Parallel to these aspects of women's lives is their sexual oppression. Women's bodies are degraded by their use as sales gimmicks (the model draped across the bonnet of a car), by their depiction in newspapers and magazines, in soft and hard pornography (page 3 of the *Sun*, and many readily available pornographic magazines such as *Playboy*, *Penthouse*, *Esquire*, etc). Sexual harassment of women is exceedingly common (wolf-whistles, touching up, flashing) and sexual assault on women inside and outside relationships is not only common, but often not treated as crime ('she brought it upon herself . . . she was asking for it').

If we now return to the story of Morag, it is perhaps easier to see how she had understood her mother's experience and how she wanted no part of it. Her mother was 'just' a housewife, a 'stay-at-home mum', as Morag described her, and totally dependent financially upon her husband. There was not the least pretence of equality in the home — he was the important one, the breadwinner, the head of the household. At the same time he used his position to maltreat his family both physically and emotionally. Is it surprising that Morag recoiled against the lifestyle of her mother? Her compulsive eating was her way of protecting herself against that fate.

FAT AS A MESSAGE

Susie Orbach has done some extremely interesting work with women in which she has been able to get to the positive meanings that women give to their fat. Of course we are all familiar with the routine of hating ourselves because we are fat, feeling loathing and contempt for what we put into our mouths, feeling disgust with our size and shape (however unreasonable all of that may be on any rational understanding). What is much more interesting is to identify what we might be trying to accomplish by our resolute refusal to be thin.

Orbach identifies two major purposes in the behaviour of the compulsive eater. One is power and the defiance of the impotent image of women. The other is anger. A characteristic of the physical images of women most often presented to us by the media is their physical fragility. Women are often shown (and indeed often clothe themselves) in garments that make physical comfort and exertion impossible. It is impossible to run in high heels and a tight skirt. But aside from that, women are shown without any kind of muscle development at all. And of course being thin they do not weigh very much. By this means the ordinary fact that men are usually taller, heavier, stronger, is turned into a gross imbalance. Men are encouraged to physical development, exertion, competition; women are inhibited from it. With that physical fragility is often shown an intellectual incapacity. Some women actually pretend to be stupid in order to maintain an intellectual imbalance to match the physical (pretending not to know how the car works or not even learning to drive; refusing to learn how to operate the computer; not bothering to understand pensions or life assurance). And then with those goes a kind of emotional feebleness — women cry rather than get angry, sulk rather than say what they think.

No wonder a lot of us want to dissociate ourselves from all of this. Some of us manage to do so directly. There are far more models of strong women about — in athletics, in business, in politics — and more of us are managing to assert ourselves as women. But this is often extremely difficult within the social and cultural context in which we find ourselves, and for some of us the attempt remains indirect. The way some of us seem to have found of trying to be powerful is by increasing our bulk, by abolishing in some sort of metaphorical way our fragility, our weakness, our impotence. Valerie was someone who had been sexually abused as a child. From an early age she was sexually active herself. She was a very big woman, tall, strong and heavy. Despite her size (or because of it) she was a considerable athlete and competed on equal terms with men both at squash and tennis. She was fiercely competitive and therefore a challenging opponent at these games. In due course the local male squash champion sought her out to play. Their games were hard fought but usually the man won. Valerie realised that in order to have greater speed around the court she needed to lose some weight. She duly put herself on a diet and began to lose weight. Her competitiveness and perseverance served her as well in this as in her sport. Steadily over the weeks and months she took off her weight and sure enough was speedier around the court and began to win her squash games. Then she stopped. Not because she had got to the weight that she had set herself, but because she began to feel less powerful, less in command, less in control. It was as if her sense of being strong, of having authority, of being someone to reckon with, was identified completely with her size. If she lost too much weight she would be vulnerable and in danger. That fear was, of course, related to her actual experience as a sexually abused child. In her sexual relationships as an adult she had refused to allow herself to be too vulnerable, too drawn in, and with men and women she had used her physical size, weight and strength to make sure she would never if she could help it again join the ranks of the weak and powerless. But with her size she also expressed her fury, which she could not yet feel emotionally, about how she had been exploited. Her size expressed the reality that she was and would be no longer a victim.

Wendy had been married for years and had delayed having a child because of her interest in her work and her developing career. The time came, however, with the biological clock ticking away, when it was time to start having children if that was what she was going to do. In fact she and her husband found it very difficult to conceive. There seemed to be no biological impediment, although various medical authorities told Wendy to lose weight to bring down her blood pressure, but this she seemed to find impossible. She was considerably overweight and had been for years. But one thing was clear to Wendy — just as soon as she did have a baby she would resign from work. In the meantime, however, she found herself another job, more rewarding and more prestigious than she had dreamed possible. She did not, however, lose weight. It began to be clear that all Wendy's anxieties about what she would lose if she had a child were expressed in her size. Perhaps there were also anxieties about what she would gain. She *looked* permanently pregnant, as if to satisfy that part of her that wanted to have a child, but there was a stronger force that made her very reluctant to give up her power in the world in exchange for motherhood. Yet she had created for herself such an ideal of motherhood that she was unable to express that conflict except by her size.

Mrs Yates was the large wife of a clergyman. More even than most women she was defined by her husband's job. Part of her role was to be professionally 'nice': kind, good-tempered, despite however else she might be feeling. Indeed there seemed also to be a professional embargo on 'feeling' anything but 'nice'. Certainly Mrs Yates did not know she was anything but nice although an acute observer might have noticed a fair number of sour comments and disparaging judgments. It was hard for her to see that she stifled her resentment at the role she had to play, her rage at the way her own considerable talents had not been allowed to develop — because of course a woman in her position couldn't go out to work. Oh no, her husband needed her too much. Even when directly asked if she did not feel angry at the limitations of her existence, she would deny it. The only way her anger could be expressed was by the biting and swallowing of food.

There are two things to be said about compulsive eating as a way to deal with our dissatisfaction and distress about our social role as women. The first is that it does not work. In fact it is an exceedingly painful and difficult way to live. Nobody can enjoy the craving to eat irrespective of physical need. It is an extremely painful addiction that has to be carried on in secret and is full of shame and guilt. Just because a compulsive eater's binge may be no more than a couple of chocolate bars does not make it any easier. There is something frightening and humiliating about the desperate need to eat. When it means a binge followed by vomiting and purging, then the compulsive eater finds it hard to hang on to any shred of self-esteem, let alone what it does to the way she feels physically. Alice used to come to work looking truly terrible, her face bloated, her eyes bloodshot, pale as a ghost. In the beginning her colleagues used to comment and ask her what was wrong, but her evasive replies and embarrassment soon made them stop. Alice could only imagine them speculating behind her back on what she did to make herself so ill. This worry made her keep herself apart from her workmates until she was leading an extremely isolated existence.

Not only is it a painful way to live; it also does not begin to deal with the problem. In this chapter we have been considering the idea that compulsive eating may be a response to a woman's perception of her social role. By misusing food a woman may be making a statement about what she feels about her life as a woman. But this issue is not in any way tackled or dealt with by the eating behaviour. In fact it is a way of *not* knowing about or dealing with these issues. It is a translation into eating behaviour of feelings. Those feelings may be any of a large range — fear, anger, envy, despair — but they are feelings that we evidently feel we cannot know about or deal with, that somehow have to be magicked away and make a reappearance as eating behaviour.

It is true, of course, that the feelings *are* hard to deal with. Mrs Yates had been trained for so long and so thoroughly never to know that she had an unkind or an angry thought or feeling that to acknowledge that (like the rest of us) she had a good many such was very, very hard. And also like the rest of us, Mrs Yates was very judgmental about such ideas and feelings. She thought they were bad, wicked, wrong. She was very unaccepting of herself and found it hard to distinguish between a thought or a feeling which has no moral value and an action which may have moral value. So, for example, she found it hard to take in the idea that feeling angry about the way her husband presumed that she would be willing to sacrifice her life and her career for his life and his career might be a very appropriate response. But she *was* angry about it and she showed her anger in ways she did not allow herself to recognise, especially by her eating.

However, there was something else that Mrs Yates found hard to deal with, and also hid from herself with her fat and her preoccupation with food, and that was the extent to which she had agreed to be her husband's deputy. She would say that of course she hadn't expected to go on working when she married a clergyman and that in fact she had been quite glad to give up work; besides, helping her husband in the parish was very rewarding; there were lots of people in need and it was good to be able to help out. At a deeper level, though, she blamed her husband for stifling her career and her prospects and she was in some ways an embittered and unforgiving woman.

None of that was easy to deal with for Mrs Yates, nor would it be for any of us. What is more, there was no way of putting it right. Unlike Emma, she no longer had her life before her. Her opportunity to develop her career was by this time over; she was an elderly woman. Yet there was a lot to be gained by allowing herself to know about her true feelings. For a start she need no longer spend her days preoccupied with food and thinking about the next meal; but also she had the opportunity to grow and develop as a person, as a woman, as a human being. There was emotional work that desperately needed to be done in Mrs Yates's life. There was need to grieve for what had not happened, for the opportunities missed and the potential unrealised. There was need to achieve a more honest relationship with her husband, to stop sniping at him indirectly and to begin to attempt to be more direct about her own feelings. Most of all there was need for her to consider how she was going to live the last part of her life and how she could use the remaining years as creatively as possible. Compulsive eating was a way of surviving, not of living.

What we have come to terms with is that we may be unable to right the wrongs of women, in our own case, in our own lifetime. We may also have to accept that we will pay a high price for taking responsibility for our own lives. If your refusal to accept your role leads you to end a relationship, for example, then you do have something very hard to deal with. On the other hand you will at least be living your life, rather than postponing it by compulsive eating.

Mrs Brown is a giant of a woman. She's been getting that way ever since she first was pregnant. She now has three small boys; the eldest is about 7, the youngest about 2. Every day her husband goes out to work in the morning in a thoroughly conventional way, and she in a thoroughly conventional (and increasingly uncommon) way stays at home and looks after the children. She takes the eldest one to school and the middle one to nursery. Then she comes home with the little one and does house-work until it's time to collect the middle one from nursery. They have lunch together. Then Mrs Brown clears up a bit while the little one has his nap. After that they go out so that she can get any shopping she needs on the way to pick up the big one from school. After they all get home Mrs Brown makes tea for the children, clears up again and makes some preparation for dinner for herself and her husband. Then it's time to get the children ready for bed. They've had their baths by the time Mr Brown comes back and he reads them their stories and puts them to bed while Mrs Brown finishes dinner for the adults. By the time they've eaten, cleared up, made some preparations for the next day and watched the news on TV, it's time to go to bed. Both of them are really tired so they don't often make love; they just go straight off to sleep, because the youngest child will wake them pretty early in the morning.

Some women might like this way of living. Mrs Brown hates it — not that she knows. She hides her fury, and her guilt at her fury, and her despair behind her enormous size which she maintains by eating all day long. Her chores are punctuated by food. She feels guilty and miserable about the way she looks and the way she eats, and she wonders if it's her size that makes her husband not want to have sex any more. It's true that her fat can actually make it a bit awkward. And besides, she loves her children and her husband and wants to take care of them. She could do with spending some time thinking about her eating behaviour. Couldn't she?

5
THE DIFFICULTIES OF GROWING UP

On 9 January Margaret came from the ward to my room.... She was accompanied by a nurse, and, in spite of looking as though her skeleton-like body would be broken into pieces by the weight of the hospital blanket draped round her shoulders, she walked steadily and unaided.... I explained to her that treatment entailed her telling me any thoughts that came into her mind so that together we could try to understand why she was not wanting to eat.... She looked a little less pinched and cold and gradually moved her body so that she was curled up under her blanket in such a way that a picture of a baby feeding came immediately to my mind.... After a pause, in response to a slight movement in her body, I said I thought that she wanted to talk to me with her body as she had done to her mother before she could talk.... Up to this stage in her analysis her unconscious conflicts about growing up had been expressed mainly through her body in such things as gains and losses of weight.

Tustin, *Autistic Barriers*
(Karnac, 1987, pages 243–5, 255)

Anorexia was the first of the eating disorders to be studied. Almost from the beginning it was thought that anorexia was to do with problems of growing up into a woman. Historically anorexia began at about the age of puberty which made this recognition easier. Nowadays the age on onset is not nearly so young on average, but it is still often thought that anorexia relates to a woman's difficulty in 'being a woman'.

The most obvious features of anorexia are the delay or prevention of menstruation and the loss of weight. The loss of weight has sometimes been understood as a way of girls getting rid of the secondary sexual characteristics which include breasts and fat round the hips and bottom. When this understanding of weight loss has been put together with an ending of (or a failure to begin) periods, then it has sometimes been suggested that the point of anorexia, its function so far as the girl is concerned, is to keep her in a pre-sexual state both as far as her hormones and therefore her whole physical self is concerned, and also emotionally. It is a way of remaining pre-sexual emotionally. What follows, then, is the idea that the anorexic girl does not want to grow up, and particularly does not want to grow up sexually.

There are a good number of aspects to growing up, as well as sexual development — the capacity to separate from the family of origin, the capacity to be independent and to make decisions. These and other aspects will be discussed later as they relate both to anorexia and to compulsive eating, but this chapter focuses on developing sexuality as a part of growing up and the way in which it can be halted or reversed by anorexia. These ideas are also related to compulsive eating.

The capacity to come to terms with our sexuality is both desirable and a mark of healthy adult development. For the vast majority of human beings the capacity to form a long-term intimate sexual relationship is the basis of adult contentment and creativity. There are, however, a good number of different ways of handling our sexuality — among them the decision not to have sexual relationships at a certain time or perhaps at all. These decisions are perfectly valid, but cause less pain if they can be made from strength and not from fear. The anorexic's or the compulsive eater's rejection of sexuality is from fear, and it is this aspect that is discussed in this chapter.

This is the moment, perhaps, to mention what is sometimes called 'sub-clinical anorexia'. As anorexia has been so much involved with medical care, it has been treated as an illness by doctors who have drawn up lists defining symptoms. This has been useful in separating anorexia from other illnesses with which it has sometimes been confused and has the advantage of giving a way of behaving and a set of symptoms a name. These symptoms include weight phobia, loss of 25 per cent of body weight or more, refusal to eat and lack of periods. However, this defines the illness chiefly for the benefit of other people, rather than for the sufferer who usually knows very well what is wrong with her. It also excludes from consideration large numbers of women whose anorexic behaviour does not go so far, but is nevertheless real enough.

As with compulsive eating my interest in anorexia is in those who are not happy with the way they use food. Anorexia can be defined, in these terms, as using not eating as a way of expressing emotional distress and having a feeling of compulsion about that way of behaving. This compulsion can last a long or a short time. The point of focus is the behaviour and the attitude rather than whether the drive to not eat goes on long enough to produce a certain set of physical results.

However, it is important to bear in mind what is now understood about the psychological effects of starvation. This point is made in *The Anorexia Reference Book*. With significant weight loss, a weight that may vary somewhat according to the build of the woman concerned, the psychological effects of starvation produce ways of thinking that are delusional and obsessive. Unless there has been some weight gain it is made even more difficult to attempt any kind of psychotherapy.

Returning to the story of Anna that was told partly in Chapter 1, Anna's anorexia had been precipitated by three events: her mother's hysterectomy, her best friend's leaving the country, and her own impending departure for college in London at the age of 18. However, her own later understanding of what it was about was a fear that she would not be able to control her adolescent experimentation, that she was in danger of 'going too far' and that she needed to put the brakes on hard. As she described it, she had as a result been standing still for three years.

Let us think a little more closely about in what way she had been 'standing still'. Clearly not in respect of her studies, since she had completed her course satisfactorily. It was in her social and sexual development that she had stood still. Anna was someone who had begun to have sexual relationships quite early. Yet for three years she had had no boyfriends and no sexual relationship. It was these feelings, these impulses and that behaviour that she got rid of by her anorexia. And in her case her self-starvation had been severe enough and prolonged enough to stop her menstruating. She had returned herself symbolically and literally to a prepubertal state where she was not troubled physically by the evidence of her sexual potential. The hormonal changes brought about by weight loss also remove sexual feelings. Even if that were not so, Anna was far too busy computing calories and worrying about what tiny amounts of food she would eat and when and where to be capable of noticing her sexual impulses. So here was a woman whose growing up had been negotiated well enough at puberty but who found it necessary to reverse that process temporarily at a moment of later crisis.

WOMEN'S SEXUALITY

Feminist writers have provided some ways of thinking further about this kind of behaviour. They point to the ways in which girls are taught from a very early age to control and repress their needs and feelings and instead to respond to the needs of others. The everyday evidence for this exists in the double standard of sexual behaviour where sexual experimentation is appropriate for men, but an equal adventurousness in women will get her called a slag or a whore. Think how many times those words appear in graffiti and how there is no equivalent term for a man. Indeed the equivalent for a man is a term of admiration, a 'jack the lad', a stud. Women are educated to care for the needs of others and that is as true of the sexual sphere as of any other. So women are brought up to respond to a man's sexual needs rather than to know their own, to gratify the man by their response, 'faking it' if necessary and not to expect or demand orgasm and sexual satisfaction themselves.

This is all a poor preparation for the possibility that a woman will indeed experience very urgent sexual needs and desires. She may very well, as Anna did, find herself extremely frightened by the intensity of her feelings and become convinced that she is courting disaster. It was difficult for Anna to accept her feelings and recognise them as ordinary. Perhaps a further element of this difficulty lay in the possibility of her sister's envy. Anna's sister was older, but much less confident and successful socially. It was hard for Anna to accept her own enjoyment and her own feelings when they were not shared by her sister.

Anna's experience of anorexia was bad enough, but she recovered in a fairly short time and had the advantage of having a history of being an adolescent to fall back on. She had well developed social skills; she was accustomed to going out with friends both in groups and with one other person; she had a fairly large circle of acquaintances both male and female; she had been out with boys and she had had some sexual experience. As well as that, she had had a lot of practice in experimenting with and creating an image for herself with clothes and make-up. When she got better she was able to resume where she had left off. It is much more difficult if a girl has never negotiated puberty at all. If a woman puts the brakes on her development then she loses the opportunities of development that Anna had enjoyed. Her fear of growing and development is so intense that it will not allow her even to embark on the journey towards womanhood.

A PSYCHOANALYTICAL APPROACH

One of the ideas psychoanalytic thinkers have had about anorexic girls who seem to have difficulty negotiating puberty and growing up, is that for some of them growing out of being their father's child is too difficult.

A young woman from an exceedingly prosperous and comfortable family had a very successful father. He was a distinguished architect and an extremely attractive and charming man. Nancy was his adored daughter. She was pretty, clever, everything her father could wish, and he was extremely proud of her. The pair had a very close, even intimate relationship, which at times excluded Nancy's mother. Nancy would spend whole evenings with her father in his study. They would talk and laugh and sometimes Nancy would sit on his knee. Only two things spoiled this idyllic pleasure. One was that Nancy's father could not bear her to go out with boys. Whenever a boy wanted to date her and came to the house, Nancy's father would make disparaging comments so Nancy very soon felt the boy was no good after all. The other problem was that over the course of her adolescence Nancy had become steadily more anorexic. By 18 she had become bulimic and her life had focused on her eating disorder.

It is not very difficult to see what was going on in this family. In some sense Nancy had become her father's girlfriend (although there was no suggestion whatever of an overt sexual relationship between them). This had been achieved, at least in Nancy's eyes, at the expense of her mother. So you might say that in the competition for her father and his interest and attention, Nancy had won. Moreover, father had played an energetic role in creating this situation. He had colluded in excluding Nancy's mother and he had also excluded male rivals from the scene by in effect getting rid of any potential boyfriend for Nancy. The results were, however, disastrous for the father's marriage and for Nancy.

Nancy in a way had got what she wanted — the exclusive attention of her father — but she had paid a very high price for it; her whole adolescent development had come to a halt and her conflict had become expressed in a serious eating disorder. She had managed to hold on to her childhood role of 'Daddy's girl', but only by sacrificing her healthy development into a woman. The pair of them were locked into a relationship that was not only long-time expired, but also very destructive.

It is a much more sinister situation when a pubescent child becomes the object of her father's overt sexual attentions. A child at risk of sexual abuse may very well choose to reverse her sexual development in an attempt to protect herself.

Some therapists working with anorexics have used methods of family therapy to help not only the sufferer but her whole family. Often it looks as though the meaning of a girl's reluctance to grow up is best understood in terms of the whole family's functioning. Certainly that seems likely in the case of Nancy's family. (Some details of books on families and anorexia are given in Chapter 10.)

Anna and Nancy are examples of women who found the transition to adult womanhood extremely difficult. It was not clear to them at the time and indeed, if it had been, there would have been less need for their anorexia. It was their belief that the feelings surrounding sexuality and adolescent development were unmanageable that forced their anorexia upon them. The refusal, however, can take the form of weight gain, rather than weight loss. Compulsive eating can delay the social and emotional development of an adolescent just as effectively as anorexia, although not in such a life-threatening way. However, perhaps in terms of peer group rejection, fat teenagers have a worse time than anorexics. Fat children are tormented by other children and fat teenagers endure torture quite as bad if slightly more subtle. Not long ago I watched a group of American teenagers on a tube in London. They were standing by the door and quite a lot of friendly and flirtatious banter was going on between them. There were several boys and several girls. Among the girls was one who was extremely fat. It was very interesting to see that she was excluded from the pushing and nudging that was going on, and also that comments addressed to her were not personal but factual: 'Where do we change tubes?' rather than the teasing 'What makes you think I want to go out with you?' The fat girl evidently had created the position of tour guide for herself which gave her a place within the group, but she was excluded from the game of 'boy meets girl' which was the reason for the group's existence.

The transition from child to adolescent to adult is not easy and if a girl feels quite inadequate to its challenge she can refuse to negotiate it altogether. At a less desperate level, it is quite probable that we can refuse to negotiate such changes many times in our lives. It is not true that at puberty or in late adolescence we deal with the problems that our developing sexuality presents us with once and for all. On the contrary, we are repeatedly working through these challenges, certainly for the first half of our lives. If we get too frightened, too overwhelmed, our response can be a retreat into eating disorders. An anorexic episode or a binge may last days, weeks or months, and it is none the less real for its shorter duration.

DAISY'S STORY

Daisy was someone who had been anorexic in her mid-teens. She had one brother two years older. Her parents had had a struggle to make a living and in the process the children had suffered some emotional neglect. Probably as a result of this the two children had sought comfort from each other and there had been for some years while they were both prepubertal a physical relationship between them.

This had caused Daisy a very difficult mixture of feelings of pleasure and guilt. This in itself would have made puberty difficult, but Daisy had two further complications to deal with. One was that she was an independent and tom-boyish girl who was not very successful at making friends with her own sex, and preferred the company of boys. This tom-boyishness is something that feminists have helped us to understand as the reaction of an energetic and lively girl to the limitations of the role of girl that has been presented to her. What is more, the class expectations of Daisy as an adolescent were that she would leave school, marry young and begin to have children soon thereafter. The model of the life that awaited her, as her mother's daughter, was a life of domesticity and of isolation while her husband went out to work. Daisy's father had a business which he greatly enjoyed running, more evidently than he enjoyed being at home with his wife and family, since as a child Daisy saw little of her father. At the same time she saw her mother as weak, passive and devalued, but also vulnerable. When Daisy's parents quarrelled, the quarrels, in Daisy's perception, were always brought to an end by her father saying to her mother, 'Well, if you don't like it, you know what you can do. You can pack your bags'.

So, then, there was difficult early sexual experience for Daisy to deal with. There was a social role that for her was uninviting for a number of reasons, but there was also something else. The father of one of Daisy's friends had exposed himself to her and had showed her pornographic magazines. This had been frightening to Daisy, then about 12 or 13 years old; so frightening and so guilt-provoking was it that she had told no one. She felt herself in some way to blame. All of this she might still have coped with, and indeed did for a while, in that she began to menstruate and to be interested in boys. However, at 15, she was seduced by a much older man. This finally was more than she could deal with and she became anorexic.

What had happened was that Daisy had grown up in an environment where having sexual wishes and feelings carried excitement but also too much guilt and fear. As she got older and those wishes and feelings got stronger, her fear and guilt were not resolved but instead increased to the point where they were simply unmanageable. She got rid of her feelings, her wishes, her sexuality, even her memories for a time, in the wholehearted pursuit of emaciation. She had felt there was no one who could help her deal with her sexuality, no one she could talk to about her fears and her guilt. Now that she was anorexic she made absolutely sure that she did get the attention she needed.

However of course it was the wrong kind of attention. Instead of the understanding and the holding that she needed, she provoked irritation and anger. She came from a family with very conventional eating behaviour. They were a meat and two veg. sort of family for whom Sunday dinner was an important social occasion. Daisy's wish to be a vegetarian, her refusal to eat what her mother cooked, her sitting not eating and not contributing at family mealtimes — all of it provoked concern and then anger, and then despair. Daisy, of course, had no idea what the problem was. I say 'of course' because if she had been able to know what it was that was bothering her, she might not have needed to be anorexic. Her anorexia was about a desperate fear of knowing, a refusal to know. The understanding of what was going on with her that has been described here only came ten years later. She did have sexual wishes, feelings and desires but her belief (and a belief that had a sound basis in her experience) was that such wishes and feelings were too difficult and too painful. She used the anorexia to abolish them.

Despite all this Daisy had not quite given up. She chose a kind, gentle, patient man, a good number of years older than she was herself and attempted to use the relationship with him to cure herself. The trouble was that she was not only afraid of his sexual needs, his sexuality, she was also frightened of her own. No matter how gentle her lover was it did little for Daisy's fear of her own feelings and sexual capacities. Inevitably the relationship came to an end.

Then even more difficult times began because Daisy had begun to lose the ability simply to go on starving herself and began to maintain her low weight by bingeing and vomiting or purging. The control that Daisy had managed to maintain up to that point was broken and the whole of her life began to be as chaotic as her new eating behaviour. Her sexual appetite, as if to convince her that all of her fears about herself were true, became frantic and desperate. At the same time the bit of her that was still a terrified child was visible from time to time when she became terrified to be left alone in her boyfriend's flat.

In all of this horror there were two points of stability. One was Daisy's parents. Despite their anger and their incomprehension, they had held on. They maintained contact with her; they allowed her to come home whenever she wanted to despite the fact that such visits were often very uncomfortable for everyone. In fact they loved their daughter as well as they knew how. The second point of consistency was Daisy's dancing. During all the painful years of her adolescence and early twenties she was training as a dancer and then teaching dance, both choreography and performance. It would not be true to say that this had been easy. There had been many moments of anguish and despair, but at the same time dancing gave Daisy some self-respect. At least she was working and that helped her to hold on to some sense of her own value.

Very slowly she began to get better. She found herself some therapy and courageously began to look at what had been going on with her. Her eating difficulties did not go away at once or easily. It seemed as though when Daisy felt again the old despair and distress about her sexuality, she would then retreat into her eating disorders for a day or a few days or a week. For example, after a long time of feeling that she would never find a relationship within which she could love and be loved, and within which her sexual needs could be satisfied without hurt or humiliation, she was contacted by a man she had known some years previously. Daisy spent two weeks with him and both of them worked hard on talking about what had happened last time in their relationship and why it had come to an end, and whether this time round there was something for both of them in being together. Daisy was initially very cautious and suspicious but gradually relaxed. It seemed as though the relationship might have a future. The man left and then within a very short time he stopped telephoning or writing. He did not reply to Daisy's letters and when she tried to telephone he could not be contacted.

This very brutal rejection would have been painful for anyone, but for Daisy it seemed to confirm everything she feared. If she allowed herself to be sexual then the result would be disastrous. Her response was to retreat into her eating disorder. By that means she could feel nothing, want nothing, need nothing. The grieving, the anger, the disappointment, the depression that were appropriate to this loss were all hidden behind a preoccupation with food and with weight. But Daisy had in fact learned a great deal and it was not all that long before she was able to deal with her feelings more directly and even believe that she was not wrong or bad for wanting a sexual relationship with this man.

One of the ways of keeping an eating disorder at hand, ready for such emotional crises, is to belong to a profession where thinness is required. We have already seen in Chapter 1 how Janet French said that her anorexia/thinness was because of her dancing and for her dancing, but that eventually it stopped her dancing because she could no longer control it. There are many dancers with eating disorders and they live in a culture where close attention to weight and shape is the norm. In a way this gives permission for food misusers to continue with their obsessive behaviour. The same could be said of a number of other ways of life — that of a model, for example, or a gymnast. In each of these activities there is a high value placed on extreme thinness and a prepubertal unwomanly shape. They are also environments which seem to confirm the very unrealistic ideas of body shape and size that many anorexics have. The criteria for what is and what is not fat are so unlike the judgments of those issues in the general population that they permit anxiety over what to everyone else seems a perfectly slim body. Dancing in particular and the dance world have often been accused of creating anorexia, but perhaps the influence is in fact the other way round — that people who feel as if at any moment they might need their eating disorder gravitate towards an environment where their obsessiveness is less noticeable, more permitted.

There are, however, many of us who from time to time retreat into anorexic episodes, in relation to our difficulties with our sexuality, without necessarily belonging to a culture which has thinness as one of its values. Difficulties in our relationships, or even the prospect of a relationship (and therefore of sexual feelings and needs) can trigger off these times. It is as though we have found for ourselves a hiding place, a retreat, a ritual way of coping, a way of managing our conflicts. Unhappily, of course, these methods do not work — first because they cause us a great deal of pain. The anguish of starving, or of bingeing and starving, is a hard way to deal with difficulties. But secondly these ways of coping do nothing to help us deal with our underlying difficulties. They keep us stuck, fixed, at the same place in our development. They keep us from growing as people. We all have, and we all need, ways of coping, but to try and deal with the painfulness of being a woman by torturing and hurting our bodies must surely be something we need to leave behind.

6
AT LEAST I'LL CONTROL WHAT I PUT IN MY MOUTH

An image came to her, that she was like a sparrow in a golden cage, too plain and simple for the luxuries of her home, but also deprived of the freedom of doing what she truly wanted to do. Until then she had spoken only about the superior features of her background; now she began to speak about the ordeal, the restrictions and obligations of growing up in a wealthy home.

Hilde Bruch, *The Golden Cage*

Over the past 15 years or so, beginning with the work of Hilde Bruch, but continuing in the work of feminist writers on eating disorders, it has been becoming clear that there is a kind of family and early experience which tends to produce anorexic youngsters — girls and boys, but mostly girls. The anorexia then needs to be understood as a way of responding to that family background.

Before looking at these families and these anorexics in more detail, it would be worth repeating some of the general points on which this book is based. First among these is that eating disorders cannot be accounted for by any *one* overarching theory. It is true that some anorexics come from this kind of background and if you are reading this trying to think about and understand your own eating disorders, this particular account may be useful to you — but again it may not. Perhaps you will have to read further and think more about your particular experience. Secondly, although it is anorexia that is being discussed and the examples are mostly of people quite severely affected, the central concern is not so much with whether the illness had been clinically diagnosed, as with the underlying 'anorexic' attitude. Thirdly, although it is anorexia that is talked about, in terms of solutions to the difficulties under consideration, it is not much different from compulsive eating. There are differences — obviously it has some significance why some women refuse to eat and others misuse food in different ways. Nevertheless eating disorders of whatever kind are a variation on the central theme of women using food, weight and shape as a means of expressing their emotional distress.

ROSEMARY'S STORY

There is a kind of family, usually white, usually prosperous middle class, which is intensely protective of its children, especially its girl children. Let me describe such a family. The girl, Rosemary, is five years older than her brother. Her mother doesn't work outside the home. Her father is a successful film producer. His work is very demanding and keeps him away from home a lot. His wife, Rosemary's mother, is lonely and devotes a great deal of time to Rosemary. She has decided that Rosemary will be a dancer and has even chosen which stage school she will go to. She herself would have liked to have become a dancer but it wasn't possible, so she thinks it would be nice if Rosemary could be one. She takes Rosemary to classes and spends a lot of time fixing her hair and her costumes and going with her to dancing competitions. She's very proud of Rosemary's talent as a dancer and is determined that it will be developed. Rosemary is also a very pretty little girl and her mother makes sure that she is always beautifully turned out. Even though Rosemary is now 9 or 10 her mother still chooses what she should wear every day. Rosemary doesn't seem to mind this. In fact she doesn't seem to mind anything. She's quite happy to sit and keep her mother company when she gets home from school. She's a very good little girl. In fact in comparison to other girls of her age she's abnormally good. She doesn't seem to want to go to her friends' houses to play and they don't get invited to her house. Rosemary likes her mother's company best and her mother takes her everywhere she goes. Of course Rosemary has to be good when she goes out with her mother.

Rosemary's mother, as will be obvious from this account, was herself very needy, and used her daughter as her companion and friend. She could not allow Rosemary the kind of independence that she desperately needed if she was to grow up capable of living a separate existence. There are plenty of mother–daughter relationships like this that continue throughout the lifetime of both parties and are repeated in the next generation. These are the sorts of relationships where mother and daughter consult each other compulsively on every aspect of their lives, where the relationship between mother and daughter has to take precedence over any other relationship.

Often in such situations it is hard, if not impossible, for the daughter to do something that she knows her mother would not like. Rosemary knew very well that her mother wanted her to be a dancer. Through a whole series of circumstances, including the fact that she became too tall to be a ballet dancer, that did not happen. Rosemary's mother has since died, but Rosemary, now in her mid-twenties, has no idea what she might do instead. In fact so impossible did it seem for her to do anything else, to defy her mother as it seemed to her, that she could not begin to think about what she wanted to do. It was as if she had never learned to want, except to want what her mother wanted for her.

FELICITY'S STORY

Now Rosemary's family is the kind of family that can produce an anorexic. Let's think about Felicity and her family. Felicity is in her late teens and very, very thin. She has an exceedingly slender and fragile neck which makes her look very frail and vulnerable. She comes from a family where her father is a successful businessman. She has one sister who is two years older and a mother, who as long as Felicity can remember, has stayed at home and spent all her time and energy on looking after her family. They have a lovely new house and it is beautifully clean and well looked after. Since she was born Felicity has been taken care of very well. She has always been able to have pretty much what she wants materially — in fact it has been her parents' pleasure to provide it for her. Nowadays she has some nice clothes, much nicer than most of her contemporaries, but she looks after them much more carefully than they do theirs anyway, and makes sure that they are clean and ironed. Her mother does most of that for her.

One of the ways in which Felicity's mother has tried to take the best possible care of her is in providing food. When Felicity was a schoolgirl her mother was always there in the afternoon when she got home from school with something to eat to carry her over till dinnertime. Whenever she goes anywhere her mother provides her with a beautifully thought out and put together packed lunch, and nowadays whenever she gets home from work there is a meal waiting for her.

This business of food is difficult for Felicity and has been for quite a long time. When she was a schoolgirl she used sometimes to tell her mother that she didn't need to be there every day; she, Felicity, was old enough to take care of herself; wasn't there something that her mother wanted to do for herself? But her mother said no, she didn't mind being there when Felicity came home, and anyway, she felt it was her duty. She wouldn't feel at all easy about Felicity coming home to an empty house.

Over the last few years Felicity has become very thin indeed, partly because she turns down a lot of what her mother offers her. Of course this makes her mother very anxious and she presses food on Felicity, but that only makes her even more determined not to accept it. She feels that her mother wants her to eat more than she should. In any case, these days Felicity does a lot of dancing and needs to be thin to go on with that.

It seems clear that Felicity is using food and her capacity to refuse to eat her mother's food as a way of trying to separate herself from an intensely close, concerned and protective family. Her big sister is a bit tougher than Felicity in some ways. When she was growing up she had rows and disagreements with her family. This won for her sister her freedom and independence so that she has now gone off to university in another city and has created a life and a circle of friends of her own. Felicity was frightened by these rows and saw how much they upset her parents. Besides she feels she was never allowed to get angry or to answer back and she doesn't really know how to defy them.

This is not to say that Felicity hasn't tried to strike out a bit on her own. She has, but it is difficult because her parents want to do everything for her, and when she does try and do something for herself it never seems to work out, or at least never as well as when her parents do it for her. Take for instance the first time she decided to move out of home and get a place for herself. She was determined to do it on her own. She looked in the newspapers and tried to team up with other people to get a place, but it kept falling through. Finally she decided to go it on her own and use a flat agency. The agency found her a flat and charged her a huge fee. However, the flat was really pretty horrible, dirty and not in a very good part of town. Within a few weeks Felicity decided it really wouldn't do. This incident left Felicity with a tremendous sense of failure. When she had summoned up all her courage (and it had taken a lot) to try and move out of home, she had made a mess of it.

It makes it more complicated that with part of her Felicity doesn't in the least want to separate from her parents. In some ways their endless concern is irritating. She wishes they wouldn't phone her every day, or at least wait for her to phone them. But on the other hand her own home is beautifully clean, whereas the shared areas of the flat where she now lives are dirty. Besides everything is so convenient and so ready to hand in her parents' home.

When she doesn't know what she really wants in all these other areas Felicity finds some comfort in at least taking control over what she puts into her mouth. She is very health conscious, and a vegetarian, and there are many things she would not dream of eating. When so much of the rest of her life feels unsatisfactory, Felicity can at least create one corner where it feels as if she is in charge.

But she is not very much in charge even in this corner, as she knows all too well. She doesn't know when she's hungry or what she wants to eat, or how much is a good amount to eat any more than she knows what she wants in other directions. She has had very little practice in knowing what she wants — even whether she wants juice or milk, or a whole or a half glass. Her mother made those choices and decisions. But she has had a lot of practice in knowing what other people think she should have. As far as the anorexia goes, she has made up a lot of rules about what she will and won't eat, and that makes her feel more as if she knows what she wants. But of course it's a very difficult system to maintain, and it takes up a lot of energy.

As far as Felicity is concerned, her anorexic behaviour seems to symbolise two things. One is her conflict about whether she does or doesn't want to try and be separate from those parents of hers. Of course practically speaking while she is so thin there is no way that they are going to relax their hold. They don't think she looks after herself properly and they are right, although they have no real idea of how badly she does. This holding on that she has ensured will continue symbolises the side of her that finds the idea of separation utterly terrifying and feels that 'living her own life' is something she is quite incapable of doing.

The other part of the story, though, is the way that Felicity feels that her life depends on the degree to which she can hold her mother's smothering love at arm's length. When she rejects her mother's food (and then the food her own internal mother tempts her to eat) she is rejecting a love that feels to her as if it traps her in a state of permanent dependency. With part of her she wants above all else not to be dependent. Dependency feels infinitely dangerous. She is denying her need for food/love, keeping it out.

If Felicity wanted either of these things alone — dependence or independence — things would be much simpler. But she has tremendous conflict inside her, not only in her body. If we remember what feminists have been saying we might also add that Felicity's mother is perhaps not a very encouraging model for Felicity. Her mother is practically and emotionally totally dependent on Felicity's father, yet within that dependency her function is to look after everybody else; that is what her life is about. How does Felicity dare to grow up and be separate? How does she dare not to?

But remember, fortunately Felicity's older sister has managed these difficulties rather well and her example is intensely important. Slowly Felicity begins to be able to feel and to voice some of her conflicts and, in the process, her eating problems. It involves a change for her parents, too, because they have to learn how to let their child grow up and therefore how to see themselves differently. Felicity's mother particularly has invested a great deal in her mothering. Can she find a way of developing herself now that her children are grown up and will her husband also be able to adjust to the changes in his wife's role, as well as in his own? They both find it painful that Felicity now struggles to express to them the ways in which she feels they have failed her. They did love her, and they do love her, and they did what they did with the best will in the world.

There are lots of hopeful features about Felicity's life, not the least the fact that her anorexia has never taken over her life the way it can do. She works and she has been able to let herself know enough about her mixed feelings about growing up, about separation and independence, above all about her mother, so that she has not had to express everything through her body. As she can feel and explore these difficult areas more there is a very good chance that she will be able to make a complete recovery.

ELISABETH'S STORY

In a way Felicity's situation and her way of dealing with it is fairly easy to understand. Elisabeth's is much more complicated. She too comes from a prosperous, conventional, middle-class household. Her father, like Felicity's, began with very little, has worked hard for his success, and has been proud of his ability to provide generously for the material needs of his wife and two children, Elisabeth and a boy, two years older. Her mother now works as a teacher, but for a lot of her children's childhood she stayed at home because she wanted to provide a secure home for them. She has been intensely protective of Elisabeth who remembers her childhood as a time of never being allowed to do anything for herself, or on her own.

Until puberty all went reasonably well, although Elisabeth now thinks that her mother's anxieties about what 'other people' would think made spontaneity and freedom in behaviour and relationships very difficult. But when Elisabeth reached puberty she began to be intensely pressured by the expectations of her parents. Her mother was apparently afraid of Elisabeth's approaching womanhood and did her best to deny its existence. For example, she would not allow Elisabeth to buy a brassiere when Elisabeth wanted and felt she needed to. She herself had only ever had one boyfriend, Elisabeth's father, whom she had met at 16, fallen in love with and married some years later. This model was held up to Elisabeth as the one that was desirable. Her daughter's wishes to explore and experiment with friendships with boys was met with fear and resistance. At the same time Elisabeth's father had strong academic ambitions for his daughter. He wanted her to go to Oxford (as he himself had not done) and felt that a social life was simply a distraction from this more serious aim.

It took Elisabeth until she was 17 to assert herself in the face of these parental expectations. But at that point she insisted on having more of a social life and at the same time continued with her studying for A Levels. Still, looking back at it, she feels that even then there were signs that she was dealing with her difficulties by the use of food. She remembers that she was unable to study unless she was at the same time eating sweets, very little else. Thinking about the insights that feminist writers have given us, perhaps we can understand this sweet eating as a way of dealing with her anxiety about whether her academic and social ambitions could be reconciled: can clever girls be sexy? Marilyn Lawrence has written recently about the way that 'education' can pose hideous problems for clever girls who have grown up in a world where many men are threatened by clever, educated women. Evidently men still marry women younger and less educated than themselves. It is easy to see what kind of a tight corner Elisabeth might be getting herself into, and how hard it was likely to be for her to know what she wanted for herself.

Still, she was managing not too badly and might have survived these conflicts without too much anguish, but sadly she had one pressure too many to deal with. She had left school and won a place at a university — not Oxford — when her boyfriend was killed in a car accident. This was doubly traumatic for Elisabeth since after a series of relationships in which she had been careful not to get too involved, she had allowed herself to become very dependent on this particular young man. Her first year at university was a year of anorexia which resulted in her dropping out.

In some ways Elisabeth's anorexia had much in common with Felicity's. Like Felicity, Elisabeth's anorexia expressed both her anguish about dependency and her need to reject the stifling kind of love that her parents seemed to offer, instead to take control of her life, but at the same time showing to all the world by her thinness her desperate need of care and concern. Elisabeth had conformed to her father's wish that she should go to university, while at the same time knowing in some corner of her mind that it was not for her. Yet it was impossible for her to confront and oppose her father. Her anorexia was in part a translation into physical terms of her need to defy him. Of course she did not know that. If she had known it she might not have needed to do it. Her anorexia achieved the desired result very effectively — she dropped out of university. By the time she decided on a different path to follow, her father was so anxious about her that he was glad to go along with whatever Elisabeth wanted to do.

However, Elisabeth's anorexia was more complex than that. In part it was to assert some control over her life by defying her father, but it was also to deny and keep at arm's length the sexual and emotional needs that had allowed her to make a relationship with a man in which she was dependent. Her dependency as a child had resulted in the stunting of her necessary and ordinary development towards independence and separation. She both craved and was terrified of her dependency needs. When she finally permitted herself to experience dependency with a boy, he was then killed. What Elisabeth learned from this was once again that dependency was too dangerous. Her anorexia said 'I have no needs', but her body shape said 'My needs are not being met'.

To summarise briefly, there appears to be a sort of family which stifles the growth towards independence and separation of its girl children (and more rarely its boys) by over-protectiveness, by intrusiveness, by not allowing those daughters enough room to develop. Sometimes those girls will rebel against that state of affairs by anorexia. In these cases anorexics can be seen both as rejecting what will otherwise stifle, and as a way of taking control of a little part of their lives (but in the end all of their lives). In some ways anorexia is a deafening 'NO', shouted by someone who has never learned to speak.

THE SILENT SIGNALS

It is this 'NO' that is the most obvious part of the illness. Anyone who has ever dealt with anorexics can testify to what a deafening shout it is, and how powerful it is in getting other people to co-operate and obey. It is so frustrating and frightening for other people that it can provoke reactions just as violent. Perhaps that is why people treating anorexics are quite often cruel. The massive rejection is not easy to bear.

However it is very important to remember that the message given by the anorexic is after all *not* that clear. We must also remember that this scream 'NO' is not the only message that an anorexic is giving (or that we are giving in our anorexic episodes). What must not be forgotten is that weight loss and not eating are also both public statements of something very different: of need, of dependency, of fragility. The problem for an anorexic, or indeed for anyone with eating disorders, is that she is caught in a very tight corner. With one part of us we want one thing and want it desperately, but with another we want something quite different, and want that with equal passion. The struggle, the battle, gets fought out for those of us with eating disorders, over food.

The 'NO' of the anorexic produces responses in other people which activate their 'yes'. As has already been noted, many anorexics belong to the 'thin' professions such as dancer, model, gymnast. One of the interesting features of those ways of life for thinking about anorexia is that they demand that a woman's body is on show. Weight loss will quite certainly be noticed in this context, and even very moderate weight loss of a few pounds. In other words an anorexic in these environments is making absolutely certain that she will be noticed. Now if her 'No' were simply 'no', then there is no way that she would want to display her body. Of course it is also true that anorexics bundle themselves up in lots of clothes, deny that they are thin and so on, but it is a very readily noticeable symptom. In other words, it seems as if they want other people to see and to know about their anorexia (and simultaneously don't want them to). And why is that? Because they need other people to say 'yes' for them. Sometimes the 'yes' of other people ('I want you to eat something; you're not eating enough; you're getting terribly thin; I'm worried about you not eating') is used in part by an anorexic as a way of holding on to her 'NO' (if you say 'yes' I'll say 'NO') and becomes part of the meaning of the anorexia. The struggle between yes and no becomes part of the struggle for power, for control, in a woman's life. However even quite short-lived and sub-clinical anorexia is also very frightening, as well as being exciting and defiant. The anorexic needs to know that even if she will not for the moment say 'yes', there are other people who will say 'yes' for her.

In the end, of course, no one can say 'yes' for us if we will not find the 'yes' in ourselves. Doctors, hospitals, parents will go to all sorts of extreme lengths to say 'yes' for us — forced feeding, intravenous drips, behavioural programming, and so on. However, we all have the power to say 'no' to life, to love, to food. If in the end we decide that this 'NO' is all we can say, then we can do that; we can die, as so sadly some women do, or as tragically we can destroy our lives with a constant preoccupation with food, weight, size. This life, this now, is all we have. It seems so sad to throw it away.

Fortunately, however, there are comparatively few anorexics who are so desperate. What many do instead is to fight out that yes and no in their bodies, using food to do it with — which is exactly what happened with Elisabeth. She had a year of what might be called straightforward anorexia. She didn't eat very much and what she ate she consumed secretly and on her own. She lost a great deal of weight and became a recluse, holed up in her room in a university hall of residence, not working, not going to classes. Finally someone noticed and intervened. She was found medical and psychological help and in the course of about six months made at least a partial recovery.

So far, so good. Elisabeth's anorexia had actually been

quite effective in some ways. Her fight to control her life had in some areas been won — she was out of university and exploring other educational possibilities. However this was only one element of Elisabeth's anorexia. Her eating disorder was also a response to her boyfriend's death and was to do with her difficulties with dependency and intimacy. Her anorexia was then partly to do with a rejection of these things, and therefore also a rejection of sexuality. Compared to the complexity and painfulness of all this, her victory over her father was not very much. She had abolished her dependency needs; she had said a resounding 'NO' to intimacy, but that left her isolated and with very painful needs for someone else. After all, you will remember that Elisabeth had been brought up in a family where there had been very little opportunity for her development as a separate, independent human being. With part of her she was terrified by her isolation and found it difficult and painful being on her own.

In a person without the need to translate these conflicts into eating behaviour they might have emerged in the form of a series of intense relationships, made and broken off — a pattern of can't do with it, can't do without it. In fact what Elisabeth did was enter into an exceedingly dependent relationship with a man, but a man who had himself had very difficult and deprived beginnings and was himself struggling with his dependency needs. He could not meet her needs in any very creative way because he had the same difficulties to confront. So Elisabeth found herself addicted to someone who couldn't really help her, but who needed her desperately and so constantly reinforced her dependency on him.

Elisabeth did not analyse any of this then. She couldn't. So far as she knew she was desperately in love. Then she began vomiting up her food. It was as if she enacted with her body what she could not recognise in her relationship. She needed and wanted closeness, sex, intimacy. More than that, with a bit of her she wanted to be a baby, a tiny child, looked after every minute of the day, attended to in every tiny detail, never left alone, held and cuddled and caressed and protected. So she wanted to eat, to take in, to be nourished, fed, sustained by good food. But at the same time she wanted to be her own woman, dependent on no one, alone, on her own, doing her own thing, not stifled by someone else's presence. Closeness, sex, another person's demands on her produced rage and hate and panic. So she got rid of what she had put inside her. She forced out of her body those good things that she had just put inside it. They had become bad, poisoning, hurtful to her. Not that she said that to herself. What she said was that she had eaten too much and that she was a greedy pig and would get fat and ugly, so she had better get rid of it.

It is clear that so far as food was concerned Elisabeth was operating in terms of all or nothing. Either she binged or she starved, feasted or fasted. If she ate anything she would eat too much. Yet this had its emotional aspect too. Either she was totally independent, isolated, without relationships, or she was engulfed, smothered. Either extreme had its good points and its bad. The ferocity of the conflict produced her bulimia, the violent and rapid swing between 'yes' and 'no'.

There could be no resolution to this horrible dilemma until Elisabeth could believe that there was more possible in relationships than these violent extremes. Gradually she began to talk to her parents and to express some of what she felt about the past. Slowly the three of them began to work out a way of relating in which Elisabeth no longer treated them either as the enemy or as a bottomless well of resources on which she could draw as she liked. In their turn they began to recognise that their daughter was no longer a child, but a capable and talented young woman with the ability to make decisions about her life. This modification was a great relief to both sides.

This exploration of the alternatives to the extremes of 'yes' and 'no' continued as Elisabeth found a grandmother figure with whom she could discover that there could be care and concern without stifling, and a boyfriend who had sorted out some of his dependency needs and knew how to be separate without being rejected and how to be intimate without being smothering. And as all this went on Elisabeth's eating disorder began to be less tormenting, less preoccupying. Gradually she began to need that way of expressing herself much less often. The omens for her recovery and development look reasonably good.

7
MOTHERS AND DAUGHTERS

We are a generation who, with every act of self-assertion as women, with every movement into self-development and fulfilment, call into question the values by which our mothers have tried to live.

Kim Chernin, *The Hungry Self*

Over the past 50 years those who are concerned with the effect early experience has on later life have increasingly turned to look at the part the mother has played, and away from the role of the father. This has not always had very creative results. Fathers and their influence have been ignored while at the same time 'bad' mothers have been blamed for all that is unsatisfactory. Feminists are to be thanked for the enormous amount of work they have done on mother–daughter relationships and for giving us a vocabulary and a way of thinking that can be extremely useful in helping us to think about what goes on between mothers and daughters. This chapter owes a lot to their work, especially to Susie Orbach and Louise Eichenbaum. (Detailed references to their books are to be found in Chapter 10.) This chapter also owes a lot to Kim Chernin (whose books are also detailed in Chapter 10). She has been particularly interested in the connection between the mother–daughter relationship and eating disorders.

MONICA'S STORY

Monica had a very difficult, troubled beginning to her life.

She had had to grow up much too quickly and had played a role in her family far beyond her emotional capacity. For her the complication lay in the fact that her father had divorced her mother and that her mother was left penniless looking after a handicapped son who would never be able to live alone. Now Monica had plenty of rage and plenty of unmet need to deal with in relation to her mother, but she also saw that her mother was herself extremely hungry and empty and that her life was very unhappy. How could Monica go off and be happy, contented, successful, when her mother was so unhappy and deprived? I think it is not exaggerating to say (as Monica eventually said herself) that she was determined not to be happy. The way she chose to be unhappy (or one of the ways) was to have an eating disorder. It prevented her from being successful in her work because it led to absences; it got in the way of her relationship with her boyfriend because it could be so pre-occupying; it prevented her from enjoying the way she looked (and she was beautiful) because it make her look and feel terrible; it stopped any possibility that she might think well of herself because she so hated and despised herself for misusing food.

Now what is the sense in an unhappy mother's misery being equalled by the unhappiness of her daughter? How will that help or make things better? In ordinary everyday logic, of course, it will not, but at one level it made good sense to Monica. To her being happy and successful felt like an attack on her mother, felt like abandoning her, even killing her. Her answer to this dilemma was that she would be unsuccessful and she used her eating disorder to make her so. She was identifying with her mother.

How could this shift or change? What could get Monica out of this dilemma? Part of what was going on, and it is not uncommon in women who have had to grow up too quickly, was that Monica was confused between the adult part of her which could see her mother's need and the child part of her which had always known about it and grown up quickly in order to try to look after it. On a rational adult basis it was true that Monica's mother was not in a very good situation. She was miserable, short of money and trapped by the needs of her handicapped child. On the other hand, the best way for Monica to help her, again on a rational basis, might well have been for her to be as successful as possible so that she would have some money that she could give to her mother. And as to her mother's misery, Monica knew rationally that her mother had always been miserable, that she, Monica, had never been able to help her mother to be happy in the past and that she was unlikely to be able to do so now. Monica would do very well if she sorted out her own problems and miseries. She could not save her mother's soul for her, although it was sad that it was so.

It seemed that Monica was much more in touch with the part of her which perceived her mother's situation with the eye of the small child catapulted too soon into adult responsibilities. She felt that she was being asked to take care of her mother's needs (and historically she probably was). What the child part of her could not see then and could not see now was that those demands were inappropriate and impossible. Neither as a child nor as an adult was it possible for her to make her mother happy. None of us can take responsibility for another person's happiness. Our happiness is our own responsibility.

CAROLINE'S STORY

Caroline's mother had come to Britain from abroad as a young woman and had never reconciled herself to the loss of her own mother and exile from her native land. She was a miserably depressed woman and again Caroline grew up far too quickly in her attempt to take care of her mother. Caroline's anger with her mother was, however, much more obvious than Monica's and at 16 she left home for good, deaf to her father's advice that she should do A Levels. She desperately wanted to be out of an environment in which her mother seemed to demand everything and give nothing. She was furious with her mother for being such a victim.

However, although Caroline's anger had blasted her out of her family home, it could not blast her mother out of her head. Caroline worried a lot about her, desperately wanted to make her happy, felt terribly guilty about abandoning her. And again, like Monica, she felt she must not be happy and successful herself. Her preoccupation with food made sure that she never felt confident about herself, prevented her from having boyfriends, reduced her capacity to work effectively and gave her reason to hate and despise herself.

For both of these women there was a lot of hate and anger in the way they treated themselves. This is often the case for food misusers and then the hate and anger that they are directing against themselves is what they feel for other people. Both Monica and Caroline were in a rage with their mothers as well as identifying with them in their pain, but neither of them could acknowledge that fact. After all, how could these two women be angry with mothers so pathetic and so miserable? Instead they violently attacked themselves.

In a way, however, they were also attempting to fill the hole inside themselves left by mothering that had not been good enough. They were trying to respond to needs within themselves that had never been recognised or met.

In reality neither of them had been able during their growing up to express the hate and anger that we all have in a good situation, let alone in a bad one. Their mothers gave them no help in dealing with these feelings and so they both learned not to know about them and to translate them into the language of food. Both of them had a lot of work to do thinking about their mothers. For Monica that had to be done with me. Her mother was simply not capable of talking about what had gone on between her and Monica. Caroline was able to work quite a lot with her mother. There was a lot of shouting and crying, but it ended up with Caroline having a much better relationship with her mother and much less of a problem with food.

COMPETITION BETWEEN MOTHERS AND DAUGHTERS

There are other ways, however, in which women find the relationship with their mothers so difficult that they resort to eating disorders. One is the whole area of competition and success. It is usual to think about men's difficulties with success in terms of the relationship with their fathers: 'Am I as good as Dad? Can I be as successful and not feel I am attacking him? Can I be successful without guilt? Do I have to make sure that I am less successful for fear of his envy?' and so on. But these issues are very much around for women and their mothers too, although it is often more difficult to detect because competition between women is so little acknowledged. On the whole women seem to find such difficulty with the idea of competition that they even deny it exists. They can do this in numerous ways, of which the most obvious is simply to refuse to compete. The refusal to compete stems from a fear equally of success or failure, but it is not that they are not competitive; it is that they are afraid of competition. Now this is not to say that women do not have great talent for collaboration. The women's movement particularly has shown that women can co-operate successfully to achieve a common goal. However, women perhaps don't help themselves by failing to know much about their competitiveness.

One of the moments when this question of competition can arise is at puberty. As daughters we are no longer children but developing young women. It is a commonplace that this often happens just as our mothers are nearing the end of their procreative lives. It can be very painful for a woman who is conscious of the ageing process really taking hold — on her skin, her muscle tone, her energy levels — to be faced with a nubile young body and a flirtatious young woman where it seems that only yesterday there was a grubby little girl. Daughters are often acutely aware of their mother's feelings and may decide that it is just not safe or possible to offer a challenge. The obvious way to sidestep the issue is for the daughter to cease to offer competition by getting either fat or very thin and thus defer the whole issue of competition.

This way of competing with our bodies and our appearance is also felt to be very dangerous because, as feminists have helped us to recognise, women's sense of themselves, their feelings, their identity are all almost inseparable from their bodily awareness. For many women their capacity to like themselves depends very heavily on how they look. This does not seem to be the same for men. They seem much more readily to be able to value themselves as distinct from the way they look. So there occurs that phenomenon that so enrages women that a fat man who stinks of B.O. will make a pass at a woman. How dare he feel that he is all right and acceptable when he is so ugly and smells bad?

The competition between fathers and sons often seems to be carried out in action, in who can win. So boys compete with their fathers to win at tennis, at chess, at making money and in finding sexual partners (just like mother). These limited areas of competition probably have the advantage of not seeming to lay everything on the line: 'Well, he may be able to beat me at tennis, but I know a lot more than him about the Stock Market.' The danger of the competition between mothers and daughters, perhaps, it is that it seems to be about who we are, about everything. If as daughters we sense our mothers can't stand the competition, or if we ourselves feel unready to take it on, we may have to take evasive action. One way of doing that is to gain or lose weight. Weight gain at this age and stage is so common that we even have a name for it — 'puppy fat'. Of course there is an ordinary and appropriate weight gain at this stage of our development brought about by hormonal changes, but our difficulties in becoming very obviously our mother's rival may well have something to do with considerable weight gain or loss.

However there can also be difficulties of competition between daughters and mothers over accomplishment and achievement, just as there are between sons and fathers.

One client of mine had a mother who was an extremely successful musician. Her daughter, Hilary, was herself talented in several artistic fields, as a singer, a dancer, an actress (but not, interestingly, as a musician). From childhood it had been expected that she would do something very remarkable as a performing artist. Her chief interest when I knew her was in dance, but she was prevented from becoming anything like as good as she might have been by her eating disorder which was so severe and had gone on for so long that it seriously threatened her health. By vomiting and laxative abuse she had so much depleted her body of vital minerals that her health was severely undermined. This stopped her dancing. The issue seemed to be whether, with such a distinguished mother and such expectations of her, Hilary could dare to compete.

Much more often our mothers have accomplished very little in any professional or career sense. This can nonetheless place a heavy burden on us, for anything we accomplish in that way will surpass their achievement. Perhaps we fear their envy, fear our own wish to do better, and that may be partly why so many women finish a training or an education and then do nothing with it. Many women seem to use eating disorders to get themselves out of training or education. It seems an awful lot safer to fail, and interestingly mothers are the ones who say, 'Never mind. I just want you to be happy'. Fathers tend to say, 'I think you should finish the year'.

THE LEGACY OF ANGER

There is also the question of the rage about their mothers that so many women carry with them. Some of that is probably built in. Mothers are extremely powerful in the lives of young children and it would be an extraordinary child who did not have a legacy of anger and dissatisfaction. Indeed it is probably necessary for mothers to fail their children to some degree, to be unsatisfactory, or otherwise girls would never leave home. But many women seem to have the memory of real and significant bad treatment and don't know what to do with the feelings they retain from those times. They have great difficulty with their rage with their mothers and often direct it against themselves. You may remember the story of Isabel who got back at her mean mother by gorging packets of biscuits.

Another woman, Susan, had been trained up from an early age to be a dancer. When she was a child and teenager her mother, who was significantly overweight, had deprived Susan of food to keep her thin for dancing: 'No, Susan, no ice cream for you. Have an apple.' Mother had wanted to be a dancer herself and it looked as though Susan had the job of being both thin and a dancer for her mother. Not surprisingly this created enormous rage and resentment in Susan, but while she was at home she was too frightened to be able to express it, although there were lots of rows about food and Susan's secret sweet eating. When she left home she began to put on weight to such an extent that her ability to go on dancing was at risk. There was tremendous secret satisfaction for Susan in seeing how she could enrage and pay back her mother for what she had put her through simply by eating the things she had been deprived of for all those long years. It was some time before she could see that, however, and even longer before she could separate out whether it was only her mother who wanted her to dance. Her fury with her mother was bringing her to destroy her dancing before she had really considered whether she might like it for herself.

One woman whose beginnings had not been happy had a mother who was so bossy and interfering that she would even demand that her daughter talk when mother thought she should. Of course that created a real game between them when Theresa discovered she could wind her mother up just by not saying anything. There was a lot of real unhappiness for Theresa which she dealt with by getting very thin. In due course she left home and when she went back to visit used to raid the refrigerator and eat voraciously. It seemed as though she was trying to express all her hatred and anger with the mother who didn't love her well enough, by stealing and spoiling other kinds of nourishment.

THE NEED TO SEPARATE

Some perspective on all these examples of mother/daughter relationships can be gained if they are placed in the context of what is the major issue for mothers and growing daughters: that of separation. The question for all mothers is, 'Can I let my daughter go with my blessing to live her life as well as she can and for herself?' The question for all daughters is, 'Can I let my mother go and live as well as I can and for myself?'

Often when people hear the word 'separation' they seem to imagine some final parting, some absolute ending. Indeed, men have often been praised for what is seen as their ability to leave their mothers behind them and go off and live their lives. More recently, however, people have begun to wonder whether men's much vaunted independence comes from an organic process of emotional growth, or from a cutting off and denial of feelings. It is becoming ever clearer that men rely on women to do all kinds of emotional work for them, and by that means avoid much of the pain of feelings. On the other hand, women have often been criticised for failing to separate and for holding on to what seems an inappropriately 'childish' role in relation especially to their mothers. For instance I heard a conversation on the bus one day where a couple in their sixties were describing their grown-up daughter, married and with children. What they described was a total dependency: 'She phones up and she's round to us for the least little thing. If anything happens,' said her mother, 'she wants me to be round to her.' It seems as though in this case no psychological separation whatever has taken place. On the other hand, recent thinking has suggested that independence and individuation for women is not and probably will never be the kind of ruthless detachment that men so often seem to practise. Women have in their growing up developed an ability for connectedness which is a strength and of great importance.

So then, what does it mean to talk about women separating from their mothers? It means mothers and daughters reaching an understanding that they are two separate individuals. At one level, of course, this is blindingly obvious, but at another it is not. They are not separate if the inner and emotional lives of mother and daughter are still tangled up together. In all the situations that were described earlier this was the case. All of those daughters were behaving in ways that were to do with their mothers rather than with themselves. They were unable to be clear about what they wanted and what was for their good as distinct from their mothers'. In a way they were living in this respect as if they and their mothers were the same person, a single unit, unseparated.

The issue of separation for women is a complex one — too complex to explore in detail here except for two points. One is that it demands from us a process of mourning and letting go. The mourning is for what has been good and belongs to a stage of our life now over and also for what has not been right and for what we have not been given. A lot of our holding on is in the hope that we will finally get what we feel we never had enough of: love, approval, whatever it might be. A lot of women I have worked with have returned over and over again to bad situations and come away battered. The revisiting is in the unconscious hope that this time it will be different: 'This time I will get what I want; this time my mother will be the way I want her to be.' But we also need to mourn the ending of a part of our lives and a stage of our development in order to be able to take on the challenges of adult life. The letting go has to be a mutual process. Separation is a two-way street, with some sadness in it for both mother and daughter.

The other point is that eating disorders inhibit the vital process of separation because they blot out feelings. This means that such women get stuck in acting out their feelings about their mothers and this prevents them from developing as human beings.

8
EATING YOUR HEART OUT

'I eat only to fill the hole in my heart.'

Compulsive eater

So far several possible meanings have been explored that singly or in combination may be at the root of an eating disorder. They have been considered as a response to crisis, as a reaction to the social role demanded of women, as a holding pattern in dealing with sexuality and growing up, as a means of self-assertion in a life that feels over-controlled by others and as a means of coping with the relationship with our mothers. However there are other ways of understanding these problems. One of these is based on the premise that both the ravenous craving that results in compulsive eating and the violent denial of hunger that results in anorexia can be physical expressions of terrible emotional emptiness that there seems no way of soothing or satisfying.

The roots of this hunger, this emptiness, are most often to be found in early experience that has not been good enough to enable a person to grow up with a full feeling of being loved and valued. Jennifer was a young woman whose childhood had been spent between her mother and her grandmother. At the age of 3 family circumstances had meant that her mother could no longer look after her and she had been sent to live with her grandmother. This in itself was bad enough since other children in the family stayed with her mother, but her grandmother was also a harsh and unloving woman with whom Jennifer was very unhappy. Now Jennifer was also a person of considerable strength and determination. She survived this beginning and used her anger about it to make a success. On the outside she appeared a cheerful, well organised and ambitious young woman. On the inside, however, there was a part of her that was a desperately unhappy and unloved child. When that part of her was touched by some incident during the day she would be overcome by the most appalling cravings and feelings of emptiness. Jennifer felt these to be a craving for food and would binge voraciously and desperately, but at the same time she would know with part of her that it was not food she was hungry for but something else.

That something else is often identified as sex. Penelope was a young woman whose parents had separated when she was quite small. The children had stayed with their mother who had remarried. By this second husband she had had other children. Penelope was violently jealous of these half-siblings because she felt rejected by her mother. As a teenager she went off in a rage to live with her father, but he too had remarried and Penelope could not make a relationship with his second wife and other children. The poor girl felt she had no parents and no home. At that time when she was quite young, only about 16, she found a boyfriend. He was a capable, successful and gentle man a few years older who was prepared to take care of Penelope. What neither one of them was prepared for was the weight of dependency that Penelope very soon began to place on him. Adam became the absolute centre of her universe. She resented his absence at work, but even more his absences when he went to play squash and meet his friends. She had an insatiable need to be cuddled and comforted and attended to by him. This need was often felt to be sexual so that a great deal of love-making went on between them. Nevertheless sex left her feeling empty and unsatisfied, wanting more — although she could not identify what that 'more' was. Adam told Penelope that he felt that if she could, she would get right inside him. During his absence this emptiness, this craving, could become unbearable amd would be experienced by Penelope as a compulsive need to eat. She would then binge and vomit. At other times she would protect herself from these feelings by total self-sufficiency and in these moods would triumphantly do all sorts of things that she was usually afraid to do on her own. At these times she would also stop eating.

What Penelope was in touch with was the painful truth that her relationship with her boyfriend could not satisfy needs that dated from much earlier in her life. With part of her she was a baby needing a mother; a sexual relationship touched on those same needs for intimacy, dependency, loving and holding, but because she was not in fact a baby with her mother, but a young woman in a relationship with another young adult, those needs could never be properly satisfied. An adult sexual relationship is not, so to speak, designed to do that job, although it can certainly from time to time satisfy some of the residual infant needs of an adult. For the same reason, and much more obviously, infant needs cannot be met by bingeing. On the other hand, those infant needs cannot be denied by starvation — or at least not without paying a price so high that it makes nonsense of starvation as a way of coping.

THE LIFE-LONG INFLUENCE OF CHILDHOOD EXPERIENCES

This approach rests heavily on the assumption that the way things were for us when we were very small and during our growing up has a very profound effect on us in our adult lives. This is not the book or the place for a demonstration of this theory, although much of what is said here owes a lot to the object relations theories of human development, in particular as expressed by D.W. Winnicott and those who have since developed his ideas. (References to their work will be found in Chapter 10.) All the evidence suggests that early experience has a very profound effect on us, for good or ill, and that much though we might like to we cannot forget about it, because it affects us powerfully all the time in the way we live our adult lives. It is as though that early unhappiness lives and is active inside us. We can find that we respond to situations as if we were still terrified babies or needy or neglected children of six or eight or ten. We might want to forget, but in all kinds of ways our earlier distress will make itself known.

For some people early deprivation will find expression in their lives as adolescents and young adults in the form of eating disorders. People who have eating disorders and come to me for counselling often ask, 'Why now?' 'If it is true,' they say, 'that the root of my problem was in all the awful things that happened while I was growing up, why has it taken until now, when I am 18 (or 20 or 22) for it to become a problem? Why didn't I have an eating disorder then, when it was all happening?' This is a difficult question to answer. It appears that some children actually do not manage to cope with the difficulties of their child-hood and become disturbed to such an extent that they become obviously emotionally ill — occasionally with eating disorders. However, most children seem to find ways of coping with whatever is not good enough in their family environment until their mid- to late teens. At that point several things happen. One is that most leave home; another is that they begin to enter into important relationships with potential partners; a third is that they make the radical change from school to college or work. This period — which might take place any time within the decade or so between 16 and 25 — is a time of great stress and change. If there is not a firm foundation on which to build, this is the moment when it will become apparent.

It is important for those of us for whom life falls apart in our late teens or early twenties to be able to recognise that we did the best job we could in surviving what was not good in our childhoods. If we need to do some repair work it is hardly surprising and not something that should be a source of shame. We did not create the difficulties of our early lives; it was not Jennifer's fault that her mother could not look after her, or that her grandmother was cruel and unloving; it was not Penelope's fault that her parents divorced and remarried and that Penelope was faced with tremendous difficulties in knowing where she belonged. The task that lies before us when our ways of coping stop working is to try and repair some of that early damage.

A SIGNAL FOR CHANGE

The sign that time for repair work has come for some people is an eating disorder. Why? Why should that symptom have anything to do with what has gone on for us as children and growing up? The answer may lie in the associations of food and eating that were discussed in Chapter 2. The links between feeling physically full/empty and emotionally full/empty are extremely close, so close that many of us cannot tell the difference between them. We cannot tell the difference between emotional anguish and hunger; we cannot tell the difference between denying our physical hunger and denying our emotional emptiness. We eat to fill the hole in our hearts. We translate into eating behaviour all the painfulness of our emotional state. So we can try and satisfy our emotional emptiness by eating food we don't want, then angrily deny our need for love by forcing food out of our bodies, then furiously refuse to acknowledge that we need love or people at all by starving ourselves and cutting ourselves off from the feelings of hunger and of need.

But why is it all so complicated? If we translate emotional hunger into physical hunger or our fear of love into denial of hunger, why don't we just do that? Why don't we just get on with it, if that's our answer? In fact some (fortunately few) people do just get on with it. They literally eat or starve themselves to death. For them the translation of what is emotional into what is physical works all too well. But for the vast majority of us, our solution to the problem turns out to be no solution at all. For a start it isn't complete. Try as we might to deal with our pain by our eating behaviour, we still remain aware of our pain. Penelope tried to blot out her craving for Adam's presence by eating, but she found herself still with the pain of her longing and the living hell of her eating disorder as well.

Often the problem for those with backgrounds of early deprivation is *not* simply that they want to be loved and cherished. The problem is that they want to be loved and cherished, but that simultaneously they are terrified that those who say they love them in fact do not, and will betray them. The meaning they make of their early experience is that their trust and love was betrayed. They think it is much too dangerous to love. They want to, some of the time, but they get terribly frightened, so frightened that they retreat, back off, withdraw, or attack and destroy. In fact they are so frightened that they do not consciously know much about this process in emotional terms at all. Instead they experience it, they live it, in terms of food and eating. They live their emotional lives in terms of food.

The pain of this way of living is horrific. It is a living torment that has no end. The despair and lack of hope that there is in such a way of life is a nightmare. Women say to me hopelessly 'I can't see how it will end. I can't see any way out.'

But I think that in that very hopelessness and despair there is hope. When people begin to recognise that their eating behaviour takes them nowhere except to more pain and more agony, then they may begin to be willing to consider whether there is another solution, another way to live their lives. While they believe that eating behaviour is the way to solve their problems there is little that anyone can do for them. But once they can begin to hear the whisper of doubt in their minds, then there is a chance that they will start to look for a better way to live their lives. Nothing changes overnight however. No one that I know has had a conversion from an eating disorder that has instantly solved the problem, but a lot of people I know have gradually and, often a bit reluctantly and unwillingly, started off on the road to a more satisfying way to live.

So what am I suggesting? I am suggesting that eating disorders are not only hell in themselves but that there is no hope in them. They do nothing for us; in fact they do worse than nothing — they actually compound our misery. We may therefore come to that point where we are willing to try an alternative that might have some hope attached to it. In my view that alternative is to begin to think and feel about our beginnings, our early experience, our past lives.

This will not be easy nor will it be painless. In fact it may well prove an exceedingly painful process. However, as has been suggested already, the pain of our underlying difficulties may not be worse than the pain of our eating disorder solution. In many situations I believe that to be true. I see lots of women for whom facing the underlying issues is a great relief. They are literally fed up to the back teeth with food misuse. The kind of feeling and crying that facing their problems arouses in them may be painful, but it is nothing in comparison to the torment of food misuse.

For those with very long-standing difficulties of early deprivation there is no guarantee that the pain of knowing about all that will be less. It may be just as bad as they fear. However it does have two very valuable hopes attached to it. One hope is that facing the past will bring an end to the eating disorder, and the other is that it is a process that will accomplish something much more fundamental: it will enable them to lay the ghosts of the past to rest. Eating disorders have no hope and no end.

If you recognise yourself in all this, it is very likely that you are going to need some help. Chapter 10 includes a description of the kind of help there is available, but let me tell you first how it went for one young woman with this kind of very difficult problem to resolve.

ANGELA'S STORY

The first public sign of Angela's falling apart was her failure to come to college. It was not the hiccup in attendance that is experienced by anyone who has an ordinary bad day, but the paralysing inability for weeks on end to get into college for more than one or two days a week. She was fortunate in a way that she was a student at a dance school. In such institutions there is a great stress on attendance because improvement depends on consistent, regular, daily work. Her absence was noted as it might not have been had she been following some other course of study. She was urged to find some help and because there was a bit of her that was frightened and wanted to get better she did.

As she started to talk it became clear that Angela's public statement of her difficulties by her absence had come at the end of a long period of great pain and misery. At this point it was not at all clear what lay behind her distress, but what was obvious was the torment in which she had lived for at least a year. Angela was bulimic. When the craving to eat came upon her she would stuff herself with whatever she could find until her abdomen was distended and painful. Then she would make herself sick. Exhausted by all this she would fall asleep. In a really bad episode she could spend days and nights like this, losing all sense of time. She would become possessed by a violent sense of anger and self-hatred — since she was so vile and horrible she deserved bad treatment and punishment. Once she began to binge and feel disgusted with herself, she was overtaken by a frenzy of hatred for herself that locked her ever tighter into her eating and vomiting.

When it was all over, she would feel physically exhausted and emotionally devastated. She would sleep and wake up feeling it had been the most horrific bad dream. But the battered state of her digestive system, the bags under her eyes, the foul taste in her mouth were evidence that this was no dream. She was ashamed to be with people when she looked so bad. Her abdomen was swollen; fluid retention made her whole body puffy. There was no way she could put on a leotard and do her dance classes. So she stayed away from school. Sometimes she would then move into an anorexic phase and within a day or so would begin to feel strong and in control so that she could return to school. Sometimes she would spend the day in bed reading compulsively so that she need not think about anything; sometimes, as she read, she would eat biscuits, not acknowledging to herself what she was doing until she again felt sick and bloated.

Not surprisingly there was very little room for ordinary life in this way of living. There was certainly no room for a sexual relationship; there was barely room for friendships. Angela had this terrible guilty secret about food and what she did with it. She felt very, very ashamed and she judged and condemned herself, and she imagined that anyone who knew would do the same. She could only be with her friends when her eating felt under control, which was less and less often. In any case social occasions very often involved eating and drinking, so they were themselves difficult. When Angela wasn't actually bingeing, her hope and intention was to eat nothing, so going out for a meal with her friends held nothing but terror for her. Not surprisingly her friends felt upset and rejected by her behaviour and gradually had less and less to do with her. Bit by bit she became more and more isolated and more and more preoccupied with food. It was at this point that she began the pattern of absenteeism that finally brought her to somebody's attention.

Whatever was all this torment about? Well, for some considerable time Angela felt that it was about itself. In other words the problem for Angela lay in the eating disorder and the consequences that followed from it. However incomplete this view may be, it does need to be treated with respect for two reasons. One is that there is the possibility of physical illness causing these symptoms and that possibility, however small, needs to be eliminated. Angela's visit to the doctor revealed a body suffering from the brutal punishment that it had been given, but otherwise healthy. Secondly, any person with an eating disorder has before her the preliminary task of consciously acknowledging that there is a problem. It is not for nothing that Alcoholics Anonymous insists on members publicly acknowledging the difficulty whenever they speak in a meeting: 'My name is X; I am an alcoholic.' Until a person with an eating disorder is able to recognise consciously what she is doing to herself, she is unlikely to be able to stop.

When a person with an eating disorder seeks help in counselling or therapy, she needs the opportunity to discover that she will not be treated with the contempt and judgement that she doles out to herself on a daily basis. Unless there can be that much safety and acceptance, she is most unlikely to say any more about anything. Gradually Angela began to be able to trust the counselling space and to allow us both to know about a lot of awful things that had happened to her and that still bothered her a great deal.

This was a painful process. Sometimes Angela lost sight of me as someone who was on her side. I became the judging, condemning, rejecting person that she was so often to herself. For a long time whenever she had a binge she would stay away because she imagined that I was going to hate, attack and despise her for it, the way she hated, attacked and despised herself. She was in a nasty tight corner. With part of her she needed and loved and trusted me, but with another part she was terrified of that dependence and really frightened that I was not her friend as she sometimes thought and believed, but her judge and her tormentor. It took a long time for that to change.

What family background had produced this much fear and how could Angela's eating disorder be understood? What was it for? How was it supposed to help? The answers to these questions emerged slowly and gradually. Angela was the eldest of four children. Her parents had married when they were still only teenagers and Angela had been born within the year. Two other girls had soon followed and then after a gap of three years there was a boy. Her mother herself had had a less than wonderful start in life which made the considerable difficulties of dealing with a baby while she herself was still not 20 even worse. The arrival very soon afterwards of other children made for what would be a challenge to the most secure and stable woman.

It was not possible to know very much about what happened in Angela's babyhood and up to the age of about 5, but from what Angela did remember and had been told, by the time she went to school she was a precociously independent little girl. She behaved like someone of 5 going on 15. From the beginning she took herself to school, went to the local shops, looked after her younger siblings. How was this premature abandonment of babyhood and childhood to be understood? It seemed probable that with some part of her Angela did not believe that she was allowed to be a baby or a little girl with needs appropriate to her age. And presumably she had come to this conclusion because in fact her over-stretched mother found it difficult to respond to those needs. Angela's mother needed this eldest child of hers to grow up almost as soon as she was born and Angela had done what she could to oblige.

But there was a further complication. The second child, also a girl, Mary, was from the beginning 'difficult' which meant that she protested and complained a great deal. Whatever attention was available from Angela's mother was hogged by Mary. Even as the babies grew a bit older Angela did not benefit. If anyone's baby needs were going to be attended to, Mary made sure it would be hers.

There was not even much to be hoped for from Angela's father. The frustrations and difficulties of his life combined to make him explosively bad-tempered. His violent rages were often directed at Angela who was terrified by him. At the same time, in other moods he would talk to Angela, then about 12, about the difficulties in his relationship with her mother. Eventually she was also the one who was told about his affair. She was, of course, sworn to secrecy. This combination of seductive excitement in the relationship with her father, alternating with fear of his rages, was not at all easy to deal with.

How was Angela going to cope with all this? She was an intelligent child with a powerful personality so she survived what might have destroyed anyone not so strong. She became the strong, capable, cheerful one in the family. That, of course, made life easy for her family, but it left Angela extremely isolated. There was no one, and never really had been anyone, who could respond fully to her emotional needs. She learned very early to take care of herself and her own needs. As she got into her teens her friendships with both boys and girls were usually based on Angela's capacity to look after them. In the only important relationship with a boy things worked out well while Angela remained cheerful and capable. When the desperately deprived child part of her peeped out, her boyfriend responded with fear and outrage. Angela's fear that no one would ever be able to tolerate her baby needs seemed once more to be proved true.

It was probably the breaking up of this relationship combined with the move away from home to college which sparked off Angela's eating disorder. Another young woman might have had a breakdown or become very depressed. Angela began a pattern of food misuse which fitted in with the needs of her family for her not to be overtly demanding. Food was the 'feeder without feeling', the inanimate mother to meet her needs. By this time she had in any case learned her lesson well and had discovered how not to let *herself* know about her emotional needs. So at that point it did not seem to her as though a lot of problems from the past had finally caught up with her. It seemed rather that she was mysteriously unable to control her weight. She was starting on the path that finally brought her to seek some help three years later.

How could all of this be helped? Well, for one thing there was a lot of crying to be done and a lot of anger to be expressed. Throughout her life Angela had either repressed these feelings or more recently expressed them in food misuse. As she grew more able to believe that I could stand her feelings, she began to believe she could bear them too. Feelings could be expressed and shared with less fear of damaging or disastrous consequences to either of us. Inevitably that meant she had less need to misuse food; she did not need her inanimate feeder any more and the strength began to ebb away from that compulsion.

Secondly there was a lot of thinking and feeling and understanding for us to do together about how Angela's early life had influenced her. It was not only that on any objective scale her growing up had taken place in difficult circumstances — that certainly needed to be remembered and pondered. What was also important was to understand what Angela had made of all that. For example, Angela believed (without consciously knowing it) that her mother had not been able to bear her feelings (which was probably true) and that *therefore* no one else could either. Consequently she had to take care of them herself. Was that true? Was it true as far as I was concerned? And if it was not true for me, might it be that it was not true for other people either? This enquiry had direct bearing on Angela's eating disorder because it opened the way towards the possibility of trusting and mutual relationships in which the feelings and needs of both parties could be acknowledged. The need for the lonely and isolated eating behaviour solution became less acute.

But there was a further and very important process at work as Angela and I continued to talk. I became very important for Angela because I was able to do and be for her a person of a kind she had never experienced enough of before. I listened to her, I focused on her, I thought about her and remembered her when we were not together, I attended to her and in so doing recognised and validated her as a precious human being. I did not do any of this perfectly, or without mistakes or lapses, but I did it better than it had been done for her before. In an important way I became a mother for Angela, since that is what ordinary good mothers do — they attend to their children's emotional (and physical) needs.

As our relationship continued and deepened Angela became more able to believe that I would be available to her emotionally when she came to see me. This had important practical effects in making her eating disorder less necessary, but it also created something different in the way Angela could be to herself. One way of saying it would be like this: Angela's mother had in some important ways not been good enough for Angela so Angela had never had modelled to her ways of being good to herself. She was as careless and neglectful of her own feelings as her mother had been — indeed probably considerably more careless and neglectful. But I was not careless and neglectful of her feelings. On the contrary, to the best of my ability I gave them close and careful attention. Gradually Angela learned to do the same. She too came to believe that what went on inside her was worthy of attention and respect. She began to be able to pay attention to the screams and yells of the infant/child part of herself.

What that meant was that although there was quite a long period of time in which Angela dared to feel quite dependent on me — and therefore vulnerable to the pain of absence between sessions and during holidays — yet she was engaged in a process of growth which gradually enabled her to develop her own good mother inside her and so have less need of me. By that time the kind of attack on herself that bingeing, vomiting, starving had been was no longer part of the way she treated herself.

At that point Angela came to the end of her course and therefore to the end of our time together, since I was the student counsellor. We had worked for almost three years, mostly once a week, during the most difficult time twice a week, and in occasional times of crisis more often. We had accomplished a great deal together. Neither of us would say it had been easy, painless or at times even pleasant. There had been no inevitable trajectory of progress. Rather there had been quite a few bumps, lurches and hiccups. Furthermore, neither of us believed that Angela was now beginning on a pain-free existence. On the contrary, she was beginning a life in which she would be free to feel her pain instead of translating it into eating behaviour. Nor had we together dealt with all the issues that were difficult for Angela. If circumstances had permitted we might have gone on longer. But in a way we had done enough. Angela was ready to leave home in a way that she had not been ready to leave her parental home. She wanted to try her wings and she had some confidence that this time they would be strong enough to let her soar.

This is all now several years ago. I see Angela from time to time. In some areas of her life things have gone pretty well. She is developing her professional career with some success. She has had some painful relationships which I am delighted to hear have made her very unhappy, delighted that she has become capable of ordinary human unhappiness rather than the grinding misery of an eating disorder. I am sure that the process of emotional growth will continue in her and I have some confidence that she will find herself a partner with whom she can have a mutual and caring relationship.

So where does that leave you, the reader? I hope it does not leave you thinking that a miracle was accomplished for Angela. It was no miracle; it was the result of a lot of hard work over a long period for both of us. It gives you an idea of just how much effort goes into trying to deal with and mend things that have not been good enough in our early lives. Sadly, there is no magic.

Secondly, things don't always go easily. Angela and I had a fairly bumpy ride together. Sometimes it doesn't work out and the therapeutic relationship comes to a premature end. Maybe for that person only so much could be accomplished at that time with that counsellor and more will be possible later. Rosie was someone who found the whole process of looking at what her bingeing and laxative abuse might be about unbearably painful. She wanted to think about it, but it was at that time just too awful. She tried over quite a long period of time, but it was too hard. She left the school and I lost track of her. Two years later I met her quite by chance and she told me that she had found a therapist with whom she had been working for the past six months and that things were beginning to come together for her. I was extremely pleased because it made me feel that although what Rosie and I had done together had not in any ordinary sense been a 'success', it had been good enough for her to feel that it was worth another try.

To dare to confront the wounds of our early lives takes a lot of courage from both parties. It is a difficult and painful process, but it has some hope attached to it and food misuse has none.

SECTION THREE

9
RAISING YOUR CONSCIOUSNESS

Anger, jealousy, loneliness and sadness will be feelings
which are frighteningly unfamiliar because they have
been buried under incessant thoughts of dieting, weight,
food and bingeing. However, it is only by becoming more
emotionally aware that you will be able to confront and
resolve unconscious conflicts.

> Barbara French, *Coping with Bulimia*

The very fact that you are reading this book means that
you have some interest in changing the way you use food.
After all, it is aimed at those who are unhappy about the
way they use food and that implies a wish for change.
However, change *is* very difficult for human beings. On the
whole we don't change very much; we stick with what we
know even if we don't like it very much. Change is frightening and disturbing, even a change for the better.

For that reason we feel ambivalent about change. With
one part of us we want it, and with another part we don't.
One bit of us thinks it's possible, another part despairs of
the possibility. Even if you are unhappy about your eating
behaviour, a part of you may be doubtful about changing
it. How can we acknowledge that and help ourselves
nevertheless to change?

In the first place we can let ourselves know just that:
'I'm not sure how much I want to change.' Those of us
with eating disorders are usually spending a considerable
amount of time insulting ourselves, telling ourselves how
bad and horrible and contemptible we are for using food
the way we do. If we also feel that we don't want to stop

behaving the way we do, or at least not one hundred per cent, then it's easy to start attacking ourselves for that too. It is kinder to ourselves, as well as more effective, to be able to recognise that any change, even a change for the better, involves this kind of doubt and ambivalence.

Secondly, it is important to recognise that inner change, changing ourselves, is not a single event, but a process which takes time and has to be worked through. It is much more like a plant growing than it is like flipping a switch. Perhaps reading this book has provided some real insights into what you are trying to deal with or express by your eating behaviour, and that sort of understanding can come as a tremendous relief. However, it takes time for those first flashes to become part of our everyday understanding of ourselves, to become internalised. If for years you have been a compulsive eater, for example, and have been attacking yourself for lack of will-power, self-indulgence, greed and whatever other failings you can think of, it is a major change of your view of yourself, your self-perception, to recognise that all along you have been struggling to deal with something, trying to express something with food and with your body.

However, if we do understand that we did it for a reason, and a very good reason, then we can help ourselves further in the process of change because we can learn to be accepting of how we are right now — people who misuse food. Very often we set out to change from a position of hate: 'I hate who I am; I hate what I do.' What we then do feels like punishment and persecution: 'Because I am a greedy pig I will go on a diet and that will punish me for being the way I am.' Hatred of ourselves is not a good beginning for our new growth and development as people.

I was talking to one young woman who had come to the point that you may be at now. She had begun to understand her behaviour for the first time after six years of difficulties with food, weight and size. She felt that she could begin to work on her new understanding of her life and experience and that a whole new way of seeing herself was opening up. As far as her size was concerned, in the process of this inner journey she had already lost a substantial amount of weight but felt she would like to lose some more to get back to the weight she had been before her difficulties began. She began to talk about this and to say it would be a battle, a struggle, that it would be an uphill road, that it would be like having to climb over an obstacle, that she was determined. All of these words revealed just how much of an attack she felt she was getting ready to mount on herself. The new, understanding, revised version of her was going to attack the old, unreformed, version.

We began to look for kinder and more organic images of the process she was engaged in. We began to talk about how necessary her eating behaviour had been to her, how she had used it to protect herself from things of which she was very much afraid. Now that she was beginning to change she was no longer so much afraid, but that did not mean that at the time her eating behaviour had not been necessary. On the contrary, she had been trying to look after herself in the best way that she knew, at that time in her life. All right, now that she saw things differently perhaps she didn't need that defence system in quite the same way; she could begin to let it go. But the words we found that were useful were words such as giving permission to herself, allowing herself. They were words such as growing, developing, transformation. It was not that she was waging war on part of herself, but rather she was encouraging the healthy, creative part of herself to get stronger. She was engaging in the continuing process of becoming who she might be.

But perhaps the whole process of change needs looking at a little more closely. Throughout, this book has been based on the premise that eating disorders are not about food, but act as pointers to other inner and emotional difficulties. Various ways of understanding and exploring what those difficulties might be have been suggested, with the implication that if you can feel your feelings, know about your experience more directly, you will not always have to translate it into eating behaviour. It was never suggested that this would be easy or pleasant; but it was claimed that it could release you from the grip of your compulsive behaviour.

Now often it seems that this is what does happen. As the hidden feelings come more into our conscious minds, so our whole preoccupation with food simply disappears. Sometimes we can even be quite conscious that this is what will happen. One young woman was quite able to say that her preoccupation with food was a way of running away. She didn't then know what she was running from, but she knew she was running. She spent three months losing a lot of weight until she was very thin, two months putting it all back on again and a bit more and was about to start on a further three months of strict dieting when she thought to herself, 'Do I really need to do this to myself?' As soon as she began to think and feel about the things that bothered her, the eating behaviour began to be less preoccupying and less compulsive.

BREAKING THE HABIT

However, for some people it is not so easy. The old ways of dealing with life are much harder to shift. So the rest of this chapter is about ways of changing your behaviour that focus on what you actually do, rather than why you do it. The idea behind this is that eating disorders are an habitual way of responding to our experience. We deal with our experience, we deal with the world, through our eating behaviour. This is how we do it, and for many of us this may be how we have been doing it for a long time. Indeed in Chapter 2 it was suggested that families very often share a habit of expressing feelings via eating behaviour and teach this way of doing things to the children at a very early stage. So from looking at what might be being expressed through an eating disorder, the focus of concern now is to look at how the habit can be broken.

The starting point for this is the idea that an 'eating episode' — that is to say a binge, purging, vomiting, starving, etc — can be directly related to what is going on in your life.

To many people with eating disorders, however, it feels as if there is no connection at all between day to day experience and their difficulties with food. It feels to them as if there is absolutely no relationship between the two. So far as they are concerned the daily anguish over food and weight and size just happens. It gets better or it gets worse for no reason at all. It is some kind of unpredictable plague which mysteriously comes and goes without rhyme or reason. The way they use food has, for such people, nothing to do with anything.

However this does not tally with what has been said all through this book: that eating behaviour is not about itself; eating disorders are not about food, but are instead the physical expression of some emotional distress. In fact it is possible to go further, and say that the day to day progress of eating disorders is a response to day to day emotional ups and downs. Consequently, whenever we find ourselves abusing food we need to think, 'What has happened today? What thought or feeling or experience that I have had today am I trying to hide from? What is it that is frightening me or upsetting me now that I am trying to express it by abusing food?'

A young college lecturer was travelling to work one day. That afternoon she had to give a lecture and she was thinking about what she wanted to say. The material was very familiar to her and she knew the group that she was talking to very well because she had been working with them for most of the year. She planned to make a few notes that she could refer to during the lecture if she needed to but felt that would be adequate preparation. All of a sudden, however, she began to panic. 'Surely,' she said to herself, 'this is not enough preparation. I am skimping on this work; I am not giving the students their due. In fact I probably don't know enough about the subject. I haven't read up on the latest thoughts and ideas. Who do I think I am to think that I know something about this subject? I really know nothing and I have nothing to say. This lecture will be completely worthless.'

And so she went on attacking herself for the rest of the journey. She was, as she said later, 'beating herself to death'. The train arrived at the station and she got out. As she walked through the station she felt a sudden desire to eat and was about to buy herself something when she suddenly realised what she was doing. It was only 8.30 in the morning; she had eaten some breakfast before leaving home less than half an hour before. She could not possibly be hungry, could she?

She went on her journey without buying anything and as she walked along tried to sort out what had happened. Not much of that day had so far passed, so she did not have to think very far before she remembered her conversation with herself on the train. She had mounted such a ferocious attack on herself that she had succeeded in making herself feel thoroughly worthless. That feeling of being nothing, a fraud, without value, had been so astonishingly painful that she had immediately tried to obliterate it with food. Hunger or even appetite played no part in the sequence at all.

It didn't take much more thought for her to recognise that her attack on herself closely resembled the attacks made on her by her mother when she was a child. In fact she could hear in her head her mother's scornful and contemptuous dismissal of her ambitions and hopes. She was now doing to herself what her mother had done to her. These thoughts and feelings were painful, but in a way less painful than eating compulsively would have been. They were also much more creative since this woman was now moving away from her habitual escape tactic and making some emotional growth. To discover something about herself was rewarding; eating compulsively was not.

This process works just the same way with anorexic behaviour. Frances Tustin has written an account of her treatment of an anorexic girl. Tustin was the psychotherapist while the girl, Margaret, was an in-patient in a hospital. Although Tustin was not involved in the physical care programme, Margaret was regularly weighed by those who were. Tustin therefore at a later stage was able to draw a graph correlating events during the therapy with Margaret's weight gains and losses. What she showed was that at each painful moment in her therapy and in her day to day life — a holiday break, a crisis of some kind — she would stop eating and lose weight. In other words, her eating behaviour was the means by which she expressed her distress over day to day incidents.

Now this is an extremely important idea, because it presents the notion of a trigger, a precipitating factor, which sets in motion a habitual response to distress — an eating episode. These triggers often provide a clue to more basic underlying problems. For example, a young woman's relationship with her boyfriend comes to an end. She goes home and spends the rest of the evening bingeing. The same thing happens to another young woman; she goes home vowing never to eat again, and starves herself for several days. Both of these women are using food/weight/ size to express their feelings about the end of a relationship. They cannot bear to feel the feelings themselves. Obviously feelings about a relationship will vary depending on the people concerned, but they are often those of hurt, rejection, anger, humiliation. Why is it that these feelings are so painful for these individuals that they have to be obliterated by a preoccupation with what they do or don't put in their mouths?

IDENTIFYING YOUR TRIGGERS

What makes a trigger so powerful? Why aren't these two women crying and shouting and getting upset? Why are they turning to food? The answer is because triggers work in two directions. They precipitate an eating episode — they trigger off another round of the painful preoccupation with food — but they also stir up memories of similar feelings in the past. Memories of rejection, for example, are stirred up by what is happening in the present. It is not only that the ending of the relationship, for example, is painful but that it reminds them of painful times in the past. There is a multiple dose of pain provided by this experience and the person with eating disorders feels overwhelmed by its strength. She isn't crying her eyes out because somewhere in her head she thinks that if once she started she would never stop. She doesn't believe she can bear to know how they feel.

So a trigger is an event, an experience, a thought that keys into painful areas of our lives and brings to mind feelings that seem to be unbearable. Now this process is unconscious — all that we will probably be conscious of is the eating behaviour. As the process which leads up to it is unconscious, we perceive our compulsions to eat or starve as coming from nowhere. In order to change things we have to be willing to look for the trigger.

However, it is possible to break this unconscious process down further. Let's take the example of the college lecturer on the train. The trigger for her was the thought, 'I don't know enough about this subject and I haven't prepared well enough for this class'. Now there might have been several ways of responding to that sudden thought. She might have said to herself, 'Well, perhaps I could do more, but I think I know enough for this class'. Or she might have said, 'That's what my mother used to say to me, but it isn't true'. In fact what she immediately began to do was follow a very well-worn path of thoughts: 'I'm not good enough, I'm a fraud and I'm going to be caught out, I know nothing, I am worthless.'

This sequence of thoughts was so habitual to the lecturer that you could call them automatic thoughts. When she felt criticised or attacked, even by herself, she would respond by a line of thinking that ended up with her feeling totally abolished, annihilated, worthless. And not surprisingly this feeling was exceedingly painful to her. Her solution was to find food with which to blot it out. The emptiness she felt emotionally she translated into a physical emptiness and so turned to food to fill it. On this particular occasion, however, she was able to stop and consider before actually embarking on an eating episode.

So, if the first question to ask is 'What is the trigger?'

the second is 'What are the automatic thoughts that follow upon the trigger? Where is the tape in my head that starts to run as soon as the trigger is pulled?' Let me give you another example. Roberta, the young woman we met in Chapter 2 eating her supper on her own in front of the TV, often felt lonely. She had spent some time at a college doing O Levels and had enjoyed it there and made friends. At the end of the course the group had split up and Roberta's friends had been scattered to different jobs, different courses and different parts of London. That summer Roberta had no job and wandered about London feeling completely at a loose end. From time to time she would be overcome by feelings of loneliness. These triggered back into her history as a rather isolated only child, living with her mother, feeling she had no friends and no fun. But these feelings also triggered automatic thoughts: 'Nobody likes me', she would say to herself. 'I'm a boring, stupid person and I can't even get a job. I'm worthless and nobody loves me or cares about me.' This tape produced feelings that were unbearably painful to Roberta. She would attempt to shut them out by going into the nearest available sweetshop to buy bars of chocolate. Now the only bit of this whole process that Roberta knew about consciously was the very last part. She knew she bought and ate chocolate bars that she didn't think she wanted. Why or how she did it was a mystery to her. It felt like a sudden irresistible urge and it took some time before she could discover the rest of the story.

Now knowing about the process did not cure Roberta's loneliness and it did not stop her sadness and distress about her childhood isolation, but it did give her the option of gradually gaining control over the compulsive eating that was so distressing to her.

The next question to look at is, what if you can identify the trigger and the automatic thoughts and you still want to go ahead with your eating episode, or feel that you are going to even if consciously you don't want to? What strategies can you use to deal with the urge to go right ahead with your eating behaviour anyway?

PRACTICAL STRATEGIES FOR CHANGING EATING BEHAVIOUR

One of the often recommended strategies is avoidance. This is not always a practical option, but for some situations it can be useful. Lots of people with eating disorders are very frightened of food, anorexics as well as compulsive eaters and bulimics. In order to make it more difficult for themselves to binge they will try to avoid buying 'dangerous' foods such as bread, packets of cereal, chocolate and so on, in the hope that when the craving to binge comes there is nothing to binge on. This is the course of action also frequently recommended by conventional dieting advice. Unfortunately the desperate craving of a binge is likely to overcome any restraint such as what there is to eat in the cupboard. Food is available to be bought twenty-four hours a day in many parts of our society: the vending machine never closes. What is more, very few people have total control over what food is in the house. In binges flatmates will steal each other's food. Those of you who live in families will rarely be able to empty the cupboards of food simply for your own protection.

Also, as Susie Orbach and many of the writers on anorexia have pointed out, the person with an eating disorder needs to be cured of the fear of food. Avoidance does not help greatly in achieving this and what is more the deprivation that is implied in avoidance ('I never eat ice cream/ham sandwiches/cream cakes') is in itself likely to lead to a binge ('I don't care if it makes me fat, I'm going to eat it anyway'). Somehow or other those people with eating disorders have to be able to use food instead of misusing and abusing it.

This said, there are some ways in which avoidance can be useful. We can set ourselves up so that when we want to hurt ourselves we have the weapons to hand. Take, for example, the woman who binges and then takes large quantities of laxatives to get the food out of her system before it can be digested. Keeping stores of laxatives on hand is a way of having this assault on ourselves always available. Some women say that if they binge and then don't take laxatives they feel much worse, but this does not take account of the physical damage to our bodies that laxative abuse effects, not to mention the terrible shame and humiliation that self-induced diarrhoea causes.

We can also set ourselves up in situations that we know in advance we are unable to handle, especially in the transitional period of recovery from an eating disorder. We wouldn't expect someone who was a recovering alcoholic to be able to deal with visits to the pub very easily, although in the end we might hope that he could go to the pub and drink orange juice, or even drink alcohol in moderation. In the same way we are asking an awful lot of ourselves if we stock up our cupboards and fridges with everything that we most crave and expect ourselves to deal calmly with it while we are still recovering from our addiction. And although eating disorders are not just about food, yet they are still psychologically addictive behaviours which are difficult to change.

A second practical strategy for dealing with the urge to abuse food is that of diversion. Again this is the traditional common sense of diet books: if you have the urge to eat (or starve, or purge, or vomit), then find yourself something else to do. What this very good advice ignores is the power of food in the food-misuser's life, compared to which reading a good book or going for a walk are very minor attractions. In this form, therefore, the 'do something else' strategy is doomed to failure.

Furthermore, although it is true that the lives of food misusers are often lacking in interest and stimulus, the whole psychological cause behind their disorder is precisely to distract them, preoccupy them, so that it is impossible to attend to anything else. Some food misusers function extremely well in some areas of their lives — for example, work — but they can't handle relationships or a personal life. A preoccupation with their eating disorder then makes it difficult if not impossible to do so. Yet other food misusers function well at work and have a social life, but simultaneously carry on another secret life of anxiety and shame about food and eating. Such people fear that they will be found out and consequently plan very carefully so that their secret is not discovered.

The idea that food misusers whose habit is this developed can find new and interesting things to do to distract them from food is to put the cart way in front of the horse. The hope is that once the underlying causes of their behaviour have begun to be made more conscious, then the need for the eating disorder will diminish, leaving space for what is new and interesting.

Nevertheless, there is an aspect of diverting ourselves from food that is worth dwelling on and can be useful. This is another point most convincingly put by Susie Orbach. Our urge to binge is a sign of hunger and craving, but not for food. We have mistranslated the signals and are feeling physically what is in fact emotional. So what is it that we need? Can we allow ourselves to know? Can we pause before we put food in our mouths to identify more accurately what it is we crave? Do we, for example, want mouth comfort, rather than stomach comfort? So do we want to suck something (a lollipop, gum, a finger?) rather than eat something? Do we want to cry, perhaps, or to be cuddled? Do we want sex? Do we want excitement?

Many of us who are food misusers know very well that we are eating or starving to fill some need that we are afraid to name, to hide something from ourselves. I don't forget the young woman who said to me, 'I eat to fill the hole in my heart' or the woman who said, 'I eat to stop myself thinking about things I don't want to think about' or the anorexic girl who said, 'When I hurt too much I stop eating'. All of them had been convinced that their eating disorder was less painful than the feelings they wanted to get rid of. Yet anyone who is a food misuser knows that the pain of the cure is at least as bad as the pain of the disease.

The trouble is that if you allow yourself to know what it is you really crave you may not be able to satisfy the craving, certainly not at that moment. In other words you may find yourself experiencing acute longings which you cannot immediately satisfy. What if you discover, 'No, I do not want to eat this container of salted peanuts, but I do want to have sex with someone'? Sexual partners cannot be produced like rabbits out of a hat. True, you will be left feeling the force of your longing and that is not easy or very pleasant. And you might cry about your sadness and loneliness and frustration, but that will almost certainly make you feel better than eating peanuts. As well as that, it will have focused your attention on identifying your real wants and needs — that is the first step to satisfying them, the first step towards taking hold of your life with both hands.

This process will be made much easier if you have support. Support is the next strategy for dealing with the urge to misuse food. In the last chapter the more formal kinds of help and support are described, as well as explanations as to what they are for and how to get them. But this is not to overlook the possibility of informal support. Food misusers rarely find it possible to use their families for support in breaking the habit. Often, of course, their families are part of their problem. Often they find it more difficult to talk to their families about their behaviour than almost anybody else. And sometimes families are not supportive and understanding, but are critical and judgmental. Sometimes, however, one member of the family can be supportive. Several women have told me how helpful and supportive their sisters have been, for instance. What most of us need is a friend or a circle of friends we can trust, so that in a crisis we can phone them up or go round and say, 'Look, I feel as if I'm going to binge (or starve) and I need someone to talk to.'

The friend won't be able, perhaps, to sort out the root causes of your difficulties, and probably at that moment that isn't what you need anyway. You just need another friendly human being who will let you cry and give you a hug. And don't think she'll be too horrified and disgusted to help you. Several studies show that very high proportions of women have difficulties with food, size, weight at some time in their lives. The chances are that she has had not too dissimilar feelings herself. Perhaps you can do a deal with someone else who you know has these difficulties to agree to help the other when she needs support.

The last practical strategy on the list is limitation of the damage. There's a very familiar pattern in a lot of eating episodes which goes something like this. We experience the trigger, start to feel something we don't want to feel and then cover that over with our eating behaviour. However, having gobbled down a chocolate bar or a sandwich, or having eaten nothing all day, we feel so horrible about ourselves, so full of despair and hatred and loathing of ourselves, that we then go on to punish ourselves and hate ourselves by eating more or starving more. Maybe we can't always hope — certainly to begin with — to let ourselves reverse the patterns of food abuse that we have established, but we can spare ourselves the add-on, the extra turn of the screw that will leave us so totally despairing.

The possibility of limitation of our eating episodes, of course, implies and depends on us being able to accept that we are people who have difficulties with food. This is not good news for any of us. We can probably feel very envious of those happy people who appear to be able to eat or not as fancy and appetite take them and who remain a stable weight and size for years on end. However, that is how it is. Once we can love ourselves and accept ourselves for what we are now, today, and not for who we will be when we have lost 10 lbs, then we will have the basic ingredient for change. While we fight ourselves, hate ourselves, coerce ourselves, it is very, very difficult to change. Just let us accept the way we are today and it becomes a whole lot easier.

10
WHERE TO LOOK NEXT

Ultimately, the decision is your own; you must do what helps you to grow. And you must trust that you are wise enough to know what that is.

Geneen Roth, *Feeding the Hungry Heart*

BOOKS

In this chapter I have gathered together some information which may help you to follow up on the points made and issues raised in this book. I would like to begin with a list of books which I think are useful. They are organised in order of the chapters to which they relate most closely in the book.

Chapter One
There are several accounts of people who have suffered from eating disorders.

Catherine: a tragic life, Maureen Dunbar (Penguin, 1987).

Catherine was a young woman who died of anorexia. This book is written by Catherine's mother with sections by her father and brother. It is a sad, but also a very disturbing story of how no appropriate or effective treatment could be found for Catherine and how her behaviour patterns hardened until no intervention of any kind was possible. In terms of this book it is particularly interesting because it shows how food was an available metaphor in the family for Catherine to use; from the very beginning she had had difficulties with food and eating which were allowed to become a source of conflict. It is also the story of a family in which there were all sorts of emotional disturbances and turmoil which deeply affected Catherine. Her own account of why she stopped eating in the first place was that she was trying to have an effect on the family situation. Most of all it is a book which demonstrates that responding to an eating disorder as if it were about food does not work.

The Art of Starvation, Sheila Macleod (Virago, 1981).

This is an autobiographical account of a period of anorexia, 20 years previously, by a woman who is a writer. It is particularly interesting in that she discusses her experience in relation to the various theories about anorexia and tries to show where they fit with her experience and where they don't. Like the account of Catherine, it is the story of someone who at the time got no psychological help, although Macleod's illness was much less severe and never became chronic.

Dancing on my Grave, Gelsey Kirkland (Hamish Hamilton, 1987).

Gelsey Kirkland was an American ballet dancer, 'one of the most dazzling ballerinas of her generation', who danced with Mikhail Baryshnikov and as a star of Balanchine's company, New York City Ballet. Her career was brought to a brutal and untimely end by her serious emotional illnesses which resulted in anorexia and drug addiction. This is a very shocking book, not least because it describes the hostility and indifference of the dance world to the emotional pain of a phenomenally gifted dancer. Gelsey Kirkland talks very openly about her life, without, I think, having much understanding of how it came to be that way, and what part she played in allowing and making it that way.

Elizabeth Takes Off, Elizabeth Taylor (Pan, 1988).

A curiously honest, moving and dignified book which tells Elizabeth Taylor's life story in terms of the relationship between her emotional life and her weight gains and losses. The second half of the book is a more or less standard diet book, but with quite a lot of interesting comment and advice about the psychological strain of losing weight.

The Fat Woman's Joke, Fay Weldon (Coronet, 1982).

This is a quite extraordinary novel which describes how a married couple dealt with the conflict and difficulties of their marriage by a shared pattern of compulsive eating. The preoccupation with food takes the socially condoned form of gourmet eating. When they both decide to go on a diet the violence and hostility that lurks below the surface immediately becomes apparent. The woman leaves and immediately tries to heal the agonising void that has become apparent with frantic, uncontrolled, compulsive eating; the man uses sex for the same purpose. A painful story.

Feeding the Hungry Heart, Geneen Roth (Signet, 1982).

Although Roth starts from the same premise as this book, that compulsive eating seeks to express some unhappiness, her chief concern is to describe the experience of being a compulsive eater. She has assembled a book of pieces of writing describing how an emotional trigger finally goads a compulsive eater into a binge. There are many beautifully written and moving accounts of terrible moments in people's lives, most of them written by participants in Roth's workshops. Through it all she stresses the overwhelming need for us to accept and love ourselves more.

Chapter Two
The Child, the Family and the Outside World, D.W. Winnicott (Pelican, 1973).

D.W. Winnicott was a distinguished psychiatrist and analyst who spent many years working with mothers and small children. He had the gift of expressing his ideas in a way that was both charming and accessible. In the 1950s he gave some talks on the radio which eventually became the basis of this book. Some of it is now a little dated, but it is also, I think, an amazingly tender and wise book. It is particularly touching on the feeding relationship of mother and child.

Chapter Four

Fat is a Feminist Issue, Susie Orbach (Arrow Books, 1988).

By far the most interesting and exciting writing about understanding eating disorders has been done by feminist writers in the last 15 years. It will be clear from what I have said earlier in the book that I don't consider a feminist understanding to be the *only* way of thinking about eating disorders, but it is certainly a very valuable way.

The most distinguished book is that by Susie Orbach. Its value can be seen by its publication history. It has been repeatedly reprinted since the first edition in 1978 and the edition given here is merely the latest in a long line. The basic thesis of the book is that 'compulsive eating in women is a response to their social position'.

Hunger Strike: the anorexic's struggle as a metaphor for our age, Susie Orbach (Faber and Faber, 1987).

Fat is a Feminist Issue has been followed up by Orbach with a book on anorexia. In this quite difficult book Orbach presents anorexia as an exaggerated and extravagant response to the cultural demand that women should be thin, small, invisible. The anorexic overperforms and in so doing not only shows her own pain but the violence of the sociological pressures acting on her.

Women's Secret Disorder: A new understanding of Bulimia, Mira Dana and Marilyn Lawrence (Grafton Books, 1988).

This is a book which tries to understand bulimia from a feminist perspective. In places it is quite a difficult book, but with a great deal of very valuable material in it, particularly since so little has been written on bulimia.

Fed Up and Hungry: Women, Oppression and Food, Marilyn Lawrence (ed.) (Women's Press, 1987).

A valuable and interesting collection of papers from a feminist perspective about eating disorders in women.

Womansize, Kim Chernin (Women's Press, 1983).

This book explores the idea that women are required to be thin because our culture hates and fears women and women's bodies. Chernin talks about men's envy of women's power to conceive, bear and suckle children and of the power of a woman's body for all of us when we were infants. Because women also have mixed memories of our infant experience of the power of a woman's body, we are also afraid of the size and power of our own bodies. For this reason we agree to follow the cultural demand that our bodies become weak, small and powerless.

Chapter Five
There are one or two books that take a family systems approach to eating disorders:

Psychosomatic families: Anorexia nervosa in Context, S. Minuchin *et al* (Harvard University Press, 1978).

Self Starvation, M.S. Palozzoli (Human Context Books, Chaucer Publishing Co, 1963).

Perhaps a more accessible place to start thinking about family systems is:

Families and How to Survive Them, Robin Skinner and John Cleese (Methuen, 1983).

Secrets in the Family, Lily Pincus and Christopher Dare (Faber and Faber, 1978).

Chapter Six
The Golden Cage: the enigma of anorexia nervosa, Hilde Bruch (Open Books, 1978).

Hilde Bruch was a distinguished pioneer in the better understanding of anorexia when it was still known as an illness of prosperous middle-class, over-protective families. It was she who described the necessity of children and youngsters having space and opportunity to make their own decisions and identify their own needs and wants. She saw anorexics as young women determined to create an area of control in their own lives.

She draws attention to the long preparation that goes on setting the scene for anorexia in this kind of family, especially the anorexic's feeling that she has to be what her parents want her to be and the consequent need always to be guessing and figuring out what that might be. Bruch suggests that the anorexic lacks the ability to be a normally selfish and self-absorbed child, so that she is consumed with anxiety about what 'other people' think of her. Assertiveness, anger, protest and discontent are all completely unknown.

Bruch also points out what an unmanageable struggle puberty and adolescence pose to such young women, because of changes that they cannot accept in their bodies and minds, and because of the self-assertion that adolescence demands. They are stuck developmentally as children.

Chapter Seven
Our Mothers' Daughters, Judith Arcana (Womens Press, 1981).

A sympathetic account of the relationship between mothers and daughters.

The Hungry Self, Kim Chernin (Virago, 1986).

This book explores the connection between mother–daughter relationships and eating disorders. Chernin is particularly interested in the issue of separation and the way in which daughters are so much in touch with their mother's pain.

Chapter Eight
Understanding Women, Susie Orbach and Luise Eichenbaum (Penguin, 1985).

This quite remarkable book is a major contribution to the understanding of women's emotional development. Much thinking on emotional development has either concentrated on male emotional development or has assumed that male and female development were the same. In the past several decades all sorts of studies have made it very obvious that from the very beginning boy and girl babies are treated differently. This book gives a fascinating analysis of the particular pressures and expectations for girls as they grow up and provides the theoretical underpinning for Orbach's other books.

Our Need for Others and its Roots in infancy, Josephine Klein (Tavistock, 1987).

A lovely book. Readers should not be put off by a couple of very technical and scientific chapters early in the book. This book provides a very interesting account of human emotional development which could very well be read alongside Orbach and Eichenbaum.

Chapter Nine
There are several books which contribute to the practical response to an eating disorder.

Two of these are by Paulette Maisner, herself a former sufferer from eating disorders, and founder of the Maisner Centre, 57a Church Road, Hove, East Sussex BN3 2BD. Telephone: (0273) 729818/29334.

The Food Trap: a self-help plan to control your eating habits, Paulette Maisner with Rosemary Turner (Unwin Paperbacks, 1986).

Excuses Won't Cure You, Paulette Maisner with Alison Cridland (Unwin, 1987).

Maisner is concerned with a different aspect of eating disorders from the one that has been explored in this book. Her books are intended to educate the reader in how to eat properly, what different food values are, how to exercise beneficially, how to deal with practical aspects of breaking the habit of food misuse. She is clear that this is her field of expertise and not the underlying emotional problems. Her response to these is very commonsensical and bracing.

Fat is a Feminist Issue 2, Susie Orbach (Hamlyn, 1984).

This is the practical follow-up and accompaniment to *Fat is a Feminist Issue*. The ideas that it is based on are the feminist understanding of compulsive eating of her earlier book, so it has special interest to readers of this book who have found Chapter Four particularly relevant to them. However, because Orbach starts from the same assumption as this book, that eating disorders are not just about eating, the strategies and exercises she suggests are very much in line with much of what has been said here. One of the most interesting sections is on how to set up a compulsive eating group and thus create a support network for yourself.

Breaking Free from Compulsive Eating, Geneen Roth (Grafton Books, 1986).

A lovely book, full of exercises to get in touch with what your wants and needs are. Also a lot of ideas on how to become more conscious of how, what, where and when you eat. There is also a lot to help towards self-acceptance.

Coping with Bulimia, Barbara French (Grafton, 1987).

An encouraging and helpful book with a lot of useful information and a gentle supportive style.

In Our Own Hands, Sheila Ernst and Lucy Goodison (Women's Press, 1981).

This is a self-help book for women who want to think about themselves and their emotional development. A wonderful book, useful, interesting, practical and full of good ideas.

The Anorexia Nervosa Reference Book, Roger Slade (Harper and Row, 1984).

A question and answer book with a lot of information.

MEDICAL HELP

One of the awful things about eating disorders is that they can do terrible damage to our bodies. Food misusers complain of a very wide range of physical symptoms which can be traced back to their eating behaviour. There are also a number of quite rare conditions that mimic the symptoms of an eating disorder and it is desirable to eliminate that possibility. Mostly, food misusers are so ashamed of their difficulties that they find it very difficult to be honest with a doctor and will usually provide him or her with only part of the information necessary to understand what is going on. Understandably the response is then not usually very helpful. It is also true that some doctors have no clue about the emotional anguish of a food misuser and can be impatient or dismissive. On the other hand, there are also patient and concerned GPs who will offer support and carry out blood tests and so on which can identify (for example) mineral imbalance as a result of bulimia, hormonal disturbances in the compulsive eater, or deficiency states as a result of anorexia.

Doctors also often have basic nutritional information

and sample menus which can be helpful to the food misuser who has lost all sense of how much is a good amount to eat or of what. In fact it has been my experience that food misusers often just do not know what their bodies need or what an ordinary diet looks like. Sometimes such people come from households where eating behaviour was chaotic. Others may have been brought up in institutions where food was provided at certain times and in certain quantities. Sometimes normal eating patterns have been disrupted for so long that a sense of how ordinary people eat has been lost. When such people have to sort out for themselves what to eat, how much and when, they can feel utterly overwhelmed.

Doctors in Britain are also the route to NHS psychological help. If you want that kind of help then you will almost certainly have to begin with your GP. If you don't like or don't trust your GP, then find another. You have no obligation to go on seeing the GP with whom you are registered. If you attend college there will certainly be a doctor attached to the College Health Service. That doctor is also very likely to be familiar with eating disorders. If you hear of a GP that you think you would prefer to your own you can ask to transfer if you live within the geographical area covered by that practice. Sometimes women prefer to see women doctors. You can ask to see a woman in a group practice where there are both men and women.

HELPING YOURSELF PSYCHOLOGICALLY

The material in this book has mostly come from my experience as a counsellor working with people who are bothered about the way they use food. Some people may want to look for counselling or other professional help to carry further what they have learned about themselves through using this book. I will try to outline the kind of help that is available. However, I would first like to describe how to go about helping yourself further if you don't want professional help.

Obviously you can read more. Susie Orbach's *Hunger*

Strike has a section which is especially addressed to anorexics who want to try and work on themselves. All of the books listed above are worth looking at. However, for most of us other human beings are what we need. Support groups are often helpful. *Fat is a Feminist Issue 2* describes in detail how to set one up, as do Goodison and Ernst in *In Our Own Hands* and Dana and Lawrence in *Women's Secret Disorder*. There is an organisation for anorexics and bulimics which offers support and information:

The Eating Disorders Association
This organisation offers help and understanding around anorexia and bulimia, and incorporates Anorexic Aid and Anorexic Family Aid, which have both been going for some time. For further details contact:

The Eating Disorders Association
Sackville Place
44 Magdalen Street
Norwich
Norfolk NR3 1JE
Telephone: 0603 621414

There is also an organisation called **Overeaters Anonymous** (OA) which works on the same lines as Alcoholics Anonymous, with mutual support from recovering fellow-sufferers. Their contact address is:

140a Tachbrook Street
London SW1
Telephone: (01) 834-8202

Their literature is available from Quest Books, River House, 46 Lea Road, Waltham Abbey, Essex EN9 1AT.

The Women's Therapy Centre
6 Manor Gardens
London N7
Telephone: 01-263 6200

This organisation runs two-day courses for women think-ing of setting up self-help eating disorder support groups.

Often those who start work on themselves after a while think they might like also to use some professional help.

PSYCHOLOGICAL HELP FROM PROFESSIONALS

The National Health Service
The first contact should be with your GP. Some GPs are interested in and informed about psychological issues and will be willing to offer you counselling themselves. Pressures on a GP's time, however, are very likely to make this help quite short term and you will probably not be given sessions longer than half an hour. However, that may be long enough, or at least enough to be going on with. On the other hand, many GPs don't do that kind of psychological work and will want to refer you on.

The first possibility may be a counsellor who belongs to the medical practice. Increasingly group practices and health centres are employing counsellors. Again these services are under pressure and you are likely to be offered a limited number of sessions. However, these will be with someone who is trained to deal with psychological issues.

If the practice does not have a counsellor then the next port of call by this route is the outpatient department of a psychiatric hospital or a department of psychological medicine. These vary enormously in their competence to deal with psychological issues. Psychiatrists are tradition-ally doctors who have had a further training in psychiatry. That training has been very largely in the administration of drugs to people who are mentally ill. However, it is increasingly possible for psychiatrists to do psychotherapy training which educates them in psychological issues, and some do. There are also clinical psychologists working in hospitals who are not concerned with the administration of drugs, but with psychology. In addition to that, some hospitals have units that are specifically concerned with food misuse, usually anorexia and bulimia. Some hospitals have family therapy departments which can be useful for younger people still living at home. There are also adolescent units attached to some hospitals.

All of these services are over-stretched and you are likely to have to wait several weeks at least for an initial appointment unless you are seriously ill as a result of your eating disorder. The entire psychiatric hospital service is primarily geared towards seriously ill people and to their treatment with drugs. You need psychotherapy rather than this sort of treatment, and it is a matter of trying to locate that within the system. Your GP should be able to help.

This does not quite exhaust the provision of counselling and psychotherapy within the NHS. There are some clinics set up explicitly to deal with psychological problems, but not within psychiatric hospitals or departments. In Oxford there is the ISIS Centre which is the only self-referral counselling centre in the country under the NHS. It is specifically set up for people who are not mentally ill, but who are troubled about some aspect of their lives. In London there is the Tavistock Clinic and the Paddington Centre. These both offer psychotherapy within a restricted catchment area via GP referral. All of these offer excellent therapy within a reasonable time-span, although you will be put on a waiting list. There may well be other such clinics elsewhere. Your GP should know of them.

OTHER AGENCIES

If none of the above seems very hopeful, there are some alternatives, some free, some with means tested fees and some entirely private.

If you are under 16 there is the system of **Child Guidance Clinics**. Some of these are very good indeed and you can refer yourself. They are part of the educational welfare provision and cost nothing to the users. Although some are behavioural in their orientation, some offer psychotherapy and family therapy.

If you are a student in further or higher education, it is very likely that your institution will have a counsellor. At the very least your **college health service** will be able to refer you.

There is a whole range of counselling agencies. Some of these are highly specific — such as Rape Crisis — but some offer much more general counselling. Three books that may help you find your way round the counselling world are *Talking to a Stranger* by L. Knight (Fontana, 1986), *Counselling Shop* by Brigid Proctor (Burnett Books, 1978) and *Individual Therapy in Britain* edited by Windy Dryden (Harper Row, 1984). It is very important that you find the kind of counselling and a counsellor that suits you. If you don't feel comfortable or happy with your first choice, try again.

Two nationwide agencies that both do excellent work are the **Samaritans** and **Relate** (formerly the Marriage Guidance Council). Both of these have developed their work considerably and are no longer solely concerned with the specific problems they were originally established to respond to. Relate asks for a contribution to the cost of its counselling sessions. The Samaritans offers free counselling, especially for crisis and emergency. Their local numbers are in the telephone directory.

The British Association for Counselling (BAC), 37a Sheep Street, Rugby CV21 3BX, is the professional association for counsellors and publishes a *Counselling and Psychotherapy Resources Directory*. This is a useful guide by area, although it is not exhaustive. Public libraries and town halls may also have details of local counselling agencies. Many counselling agencies (as opposed to individual counsellors) are supported by public or charitable money and consequently either do not charge, charge nominal sums or charge according to a means tested scale.

The work done by counselling agencies is usually short term and problem-solving in its approach. A more long term approach is offered by psychotherapy. There is not yet, although by 1992 there will be, an umbrella organisation for psychotherapists in this country. For this reason there is no one organisation to which you can be directed. You should beware of choosing a psychotherapist from an advertisement or from the *Yellow Pages*. Most reputable training organisations forbid their members to advertise. However, here are some organisations which you can approach:

The Womens Therapy Centre, 6 Manor Gardens, London N7, has a referral service for individual psychotherapy and also runs workshops and groups for women with eating disorders.

Vector. From spring 1989, the author of this book will be opening a therapy centre with some other therapists, offering workshops and courses to those with eating disorders. For further information write to:

Vector
12 Boscastle Road
London NW5

The British Association of Psychotherapists runs a clinic offering low-cost therapy.
121 Hendon Lane
London N3
Telephone: 01-346 1747

The Guild of Psychotherapists offers a country-wide referral service.
19b Thornton Hill
London SW19 4HU.

People with eating disorders nearly always have serious difficulties in liking the way they look. Interest is growing in how Dance Movement Therapy can help with these difficulties. Jasmine Pasch has done some work of this kind in workshops. To contact her and other dance movement therapists write to:

The Association for Dance Movement Therapy
Flat 3
24a Clapham Road
London SW9 0JG.